WITHI

ENDORSEMENTS

"You may feel like your life is out of your control—that others, or your circumstances or past mistakes have already determined your destiny. I've learned, however, that you have the ability to improve your life by making choices that are authentic to your personality and your priorities. Joel's book, *Finding Your Voice*, will help you tune into what really matters to you so you can make better choices and achieve goals that are meaningful to you."

DARREN HARDY, publisher of *SUCCESS Magazine* and *New York Times* bestselling author of *The Compound Effect*

"If you aren't honest with yourself, how can you be real with anyone else? You can't! That's why, in his new book, Joel Boggess guides you through the process of cutting away the expectations, past hurts, and mistaken beliefs that are keeping you from being your best. Stop pretending to be what others want. Read *Finding Your Voice* and learn how to be yourself."

MEL ROBBINS, host of *The Mel Robbins Show* and author of *Stop Saying You're Fine*

"I spent so many years of my life trying to find my voice; how I wish Joel's book was around then. If you find yourself struggling to embrace your value, may I recommend *Finding Your Voice* as a quick-start into a place of wholeness and worth."

PATSY CLAIRMONT, author and speaker

"You are doing something special for others and yourself by reading *Finding Your Voice*! The investment of your time will come back multiplied with more confidence and enthusiasm—and you'll discover a powerful voice that will inspire and encourage others along the way."

DAN MILLER, bestselling author and life coach

"With *Finding Your Voice*, Joel Boggess joins the ranks of those legendary mentors, speakers, and authors who have transformed the lives of multitudes. His profound insights are anchored by the transcendent reality that the voice is the sound of the soul, possessing limitless power to influence ourselves as well as others. Voice can elevate or degrade, it can inspire and oppress, and it can harm or heal, but, above all, it is the unique sound that enables each of us to impact our world. With the author's wise counsel consecrated to the cause of growth and success, every reader can anticipate colossal return on investment from this insightful and practical book."

RABBI DANIEL LAPIN, author of *Thou Shall Prosper: The 10 Commandments for Making Money*

"In *Finding Your Voice*, Joel Boggess explains that it isn't selfish to focus on your needs and dreams. Being your best possible self benefits everyone around you! Read this book with a pen. Your world will thank you."

CARRIE WILKERSON, author of *The Barefoot Executive: The Ultimate Guide to Financial Freedom and Being Your Own Boss*

"In this terrific book, we learn not only why *Finding Your Voice* is so important to living a successful life; the author also takes us through a step-by-step tutorial on exactly how to do it. This is foundational in terms of doing what you love and living with joy. Great job, Joel!"

BOB BURG, coauthor of *The Go-Giver*

"*Finding Your Voice* isn't a superficial fix. It digs deep to help you get to the root of the problems you're facing so you can experience real healing and growth."

JENNIFER MAGGIO, CEO/founder of
The Life of a Single Mom Ministries

"In *Finding Your Voice*, you'll learn how Joel Boggess turned tragedy into triumph and how you can use authenticity to become your best self. Reading this book is like having coffee with a friend who only wants the best for you. I recommend it."

MARK SANBORN, award-winning speaker and bestselling author
of *The Fred Factor* and *You Don't Need a Title to Be a Leader*

"*Finding Your Voice* opens the gateway to our personal power as it guides us with practical and soulful insight to our own awakening. Coach, sage and teacher, Joel Boggess is a master at leading us into the unique interior of the self for true transformation. Joel's personal story and that of his clients uplifts us and shows us how to create the same success, inner strength and joy as we live out our limitless self."

DR JO ANNE WHITE, author, speaker, and host
of *Power Your Life* Radio and TV

"If you feel stuck in your career—or in life in general—read *Finding Your Voice*. Joel's guidance will put you on a better path."

JOE CALLOWAY, author of *Becoming a Category of One* and *Be the Best at What Matters Most*

"If your life is in transition, if you have hit a roadblock and do not know where to step next, *Finding Your Voice* is the book for you! Joel teaches us all how to move step by step towards the future we dream of while guiding us through life changing practical applications that we can take ahold of and apply to our lives today."

JENNIFER FINNEGAN-POOL, founder and
executive director of Single Momm

"If your life is in transition, you need to read *Finding Your Voice*! It will prepare you to make smart steps toward a bright future."

TOM ZIGLAR, CEO and proud son of Zig Ziglar

"Joel takes you through thought-provoking questions and challenges you to look deeper and come out more alive and stronger. Too often we have been unwilling to discover the "whys." Thank you, Joel, for sharing your story and countless others that will inspire us to find our voice."

MISTY HONNOLD, executive director of M.O.M., a ministry equipping single moms to overcome mountains

"Every life has something important and beautiful to say to the world, but not every life has found its own voice. Discovering who you truly are, your offering to the world, and bringing it to its purest form is not easy. It is a process, a journey in which we need others to help us find clarity and courage. Joel Boggess offers this to you in his book, *Finding Your Voice*."

GARY BARKALOW, author of *It's Your Call: What Are You Doing Here*, founder, The Noble Heart

"In a world filled with noise and distractions, *Finding Your Voice* will help you tune into what really matters to you. This practical book will lead you back to the person you were created to be."

JOHN MILLER, author of *QBQ*

"Are you saying *yes* when you really mean *no*? Are you letting other people's dreams take precedence over your own? Let Joel Boggess's latest book, *Finding Your Voice*, empower you to speak up for yourself and claim the life you want."

ALLYSON LEWIS, time strategist and author of *The 7 Minute Solution*

"Joel Boggess is a true student of self-development and success. Over the years he's gleaned from some of the most prolific thought leaders on the planet. In this book he shares the best of the best for becoming the person you were designed to be!"

RORY VADEN, cofounder of Southwestern Consulting and
New York Times bestselling author of *Take the Stairs*

"If you feel like you aren't the person you used to be—or the person you want to be—know this: You're still in there. I promise! This book will help you rediscover the real you."

DEBY and KIRK DEARMAN, singer/songwriters
and pioneers of worship and the arts

"*Finding Your Voice* is a powerful, practical book in which Joel Boggess opens his heart and shares his own struggles along with real-life examples of the growth and success his clients have achieved to help you discover your own authentic voice and claim the life you want. Read *Finding Your Voice* and learn to express your true self."

JIM DONOVAN, author of *52 Ways to a Happier Life*

"Wow! Talk about the right book for the right time. *Finding Your Voice* is a book about discovering your identity and finding the life you were born to live. I define *identity* as knowing who God is, knowing what He has already done, and knowing who He made you to be. In a day in which *USA Today* tells us 90 percent of people don't know their purpose, Joel Boggess has given us a book to help us step into our destiny. Many people in life limit their potential by unwittingly submitting to subconscious self-limiting beliefs. Joel not only helps you identify them, but shows you the keys to overcome them and reach your full capacity. *Finding Your Voice* is a narrative to unfold your God-given greatness. Read it and live in abundance."

RON MCINTOSH, president, Ron McIntosh Ministries
and I.M.P.A.C.T. (a church leadership coaching
ministry), and author of *The Greatest Secret*

"Layer by layer, Joel helps you unwrap your passion, discover your purpose, and find the authentic voice within. Once you know what makes your heart sing, you'll be sharing your song with the world."

KAREN PUTZ, passion coach, speaker, and coauthor
of *Gliding Soles: Lessons from a Life on Water*

"Who am I? What do I really want? Those two questions plague humanity. In *Finding Your Voice*, Joel Boggess takes you on his own personal journey to show you how he found *his* voice. Along the way, he masterfully shows you how you can find yours as well. Plus, once you find it, Joel teaches you how to listen to your voice, regardless of what the rest of the world is saying, so you can live your purpose."

URSULA MENTJES, bestselling author of *Selling with Intention* and founder of salescoachnow.com

"A good book—for me—is one in which the author's story and message(s) are strong in their own right, but also cause the reader to examine their own story and the actions they take from that position. It's through this process that we identify changes in our thinking and action to create greater levels of happiness and fulfillment in our lives. *Finding Your Voice* does just that!"

DANNY BADER, inspirational speaker, coach, and
author of *Back from Heaven's Front Porch*

"Are you tired of feeling overwhelmed or under-challenged? Are you worried that "this" is all there is to life? Do you wish you could make a change but don't know where to begin? Start by reading *Finding Your Voice*. In it, Joel Boggess shines a light of hope that your future can be all you desire—and more!"

SHAWN DOYLE, CSP, professional speaker and
trainer, author of *Jumpstart Your Motivation*

"In *Finding Your Voice*, Joel Boggess shares his heart and expertise, encouraging you to express your true self."

JAN COATES, international speaker
and author of *Attitude-inize*

"Are you trying to be too many things to too many people? Do you feel stretched thin or stressed out? If so, throw aside the superwoman/superman cape! I know you will appreciate Joel's message in *Finding Your Voice*. He shows you how to get clear on your purpose and focus on what really matters to you. Do yourself a favor: take ACTION and read it!"

JEN MCDONOUGH (a.k.a. The Iron Jen)
author of *Living Beyond Rich*

"In *Finding Your Voice*, Joel Boggess walks you through the process of what it takes to truly live an authentic and meaningful life. Make no mistake, you were meant for greatness, and in the pages of this book you will find the tools necessary to unleash your greatness."

JOSH HINDS, speaker and
author of *It's Your Life, LIVE BIG!*

"In a world of conformity, where many are looking to blend, Joel steps forward and shows us how to be unique. *Finding Your Voice* coaches us to find our God-given uniqueness and excel! The women I serve will be enlightened by this approach."

VICKI HARVEY-HELGESEN, executive director
of Leaving The Cocoon

"Joel Boggess's message and principles that he shares in this book are life changing. Joel will help you find and strengthen your own voice that will challenge you to go after your passion. Make the commitment to yourself to pick up a copy of *Finding Your Voice*, read it and take action. It is an amazing tool to help you reach the levels of success that you are looking to achieve."

RYAN C. LOWE, speaker and
author of *Get Off Your Attitude*

"Life's journey would be easier if it came with GPS directions. Since that *isn't* how life works, the next best thing you can do is to find and follow your voice—the truth about who you are and what you care about. In *Finding Your Voice*, Joel Boggess provides guidance to help you map your own journey for a meaningful and fulfilling life."

BERNIE SIEGEL, MD, author of *Faith, Hope &*
Healing and *365 Prescriptions for the Soul*

"What have you always dreamed of doing? What is holding you back? If you tired of wishing and hoping, read *Finding Your Voice* by Joel Boggess and learn how to create the life you've dreamed of."

TONY AND ALISA DILORENZO, relationship experts
and founders of One Extraordinary Marriage

How would you feel if you could take your past and use it to pave the path to your success? Joel Boggess, life coach and author of *Finding Your Voice*, is your personal guide to discovering the authentic you that rises from the ashes of your past like the phoenix rising. Take his hand and step up and into your dreams. It's waiting for you."

CHERYL MALONEY, talk show host, coach, speaker,
and author of *Simple Steps for Starting Over*

"Being an artist, musician, and producer, I understand the importance of having a voice. Finding your voice is a very mindful process. The first step toward creativity and happiness is getting in touch with who you really are. If you've lost yourself in the busyness of life, Joel Boggess will help you find your way back. The message of *Finding Your Voice* will cuts through life's clutter so you can rediscover what's really important—you.

CHAD JEFFERS, author of *25 Notes for the Successful Musician*

"If you're ready to let go of what's holding you back in life and you want to connect with your passion and purpose than you need to read Joel Boggess' brilliant new book *Finding Your Voice*. Joel has done an amazing job at sharing practical and actionable advice for living a vibrant life with clarity and intention."

VANESSA HALLOUM, author of *The 5 Feminine Power Virtues*

"If you've ever sat down and asked yourself the questions "Who am I, and why am I here?" then Joel Boggess' book is a must-read. In it, he eloquently weaves a tale of his own past experiences to relay a powerful message about finding yourself, letting go of others opinions, and becoming, once and for all, who God specifically created you to be. If you want your life to be dramatically changed, read this book and let it take you on a journey that will shift your perception from who you think you are to who you really are".

GORDON BANKS, former Dallas Cowboy, author, and senior pastor Overcomer Covenant Church

"Everyone has a story to tell, a gift to share, or a message to relate. Unfortunately, too many people don't express themselves for fear of what others will think or that they'll make a mistake. In *Finding Your Voice,* Joel Boggess offers guidance for how to get past those fears so you can share your best self with the world. Read it... and then express your voice."

MICHELLE PRINCE best-selling author, Zig Ziglar Motivational Speaker, and America's Productivity Coach

"God has created every human being with a unique identity and purpose. So many people struggle in their ability to see clearly who they really are, as the inputs and experiences of life muddy the waters, and make clarity almost impossible. This 'identity crisis' paralyzes people from becoming all God intended them to be. In *Finding Your Voice*, Joel Boggess offers powerful insights, but more importantly effective processes that will unleash the potential and greatness in the reader. Rediscover who you really are in *Finding Your Voice*."

BRIAN HOLMES, author of *The Ties that Bind*

"For a culture plagued with fitting in, keeping up, and looking good, Joel's book is a beacon of light. He helps you reach deep inside to find your voice—your authentic voice—so you, too, can live a life of passion, excitement, and meaning."

KIM HODOUS, best-selling author of
Show Up, Be Bold, Play Big

"Joel Boggess gives you a step-by-step method for stripping away your masks and presenting your authentic self. I love the 'Questions for Reflection' that are peppered throughout the book. Sample: 'Are you trying to change your personality to fit what the world considers successful?' Engage with these. They will serve you well."

DR. SRIKUMAR RAO, TED
speaker and author of *Happiness at Work*

"If you've been struggling to create 'work/life balance,' you need to read *Finding Your Voice* and free yourself from what Joel Boggess calls 'the myth of mediocrity.' You'll learn why focus is far more potent than balance when it comes to creating a life you love."

CHRIS LOCURTO, vice president
and speaker at Dave Ramsey's organization

FINDING YOUR VOICE

Sort through the clutter
and discover:

- ✔ CLARITY
- ✔ CONFIDENCE
- ✔ DIRECTION

JOEL BOGGESS

The go-to guy for Clarity, Confidence, and Direction.™

Sound Wisdom
167 Walnut Bottom Road
Shippensburg, PA 17257

For more information on foreign distribution, call 717-530-2122.
Reach us on the Internet: www.soundwisdom.com.

This book and all other Sound Wisdom books are available at bookstores and distributors worldwide.

ISBN 13 TP: 978-1-937879-30-3
ISBN 13 Ebook: 978-1-937879-31-0

For Worldwide Distribution, Printed in the U.S.A.
1 2 3 4 5 6 7 8 9 10 / 16 15 14 13

DEDICATION

This book is dedicated to my four greatest teachers:

Jay Boggess, my dad. From you, I learned to explore, experiment, and reach.

Nancy Mansfield, my mom. From you, I learned the value of love, patience, and gratitude.

Pei Kang, my wife. From you, I learned gentleness, kindness, and temperance.

My clients. From you I learned how to be a better friend, teacher, and coach.

CONTENTS

FOREWORD

When I was just thirteen years old, a little recording called *The Strangest Secret* made a dramatic impact on my life. The message presented was essentially the principle: "as a man thinks in his heart, so is he." I learned the power of feeding my mind positive, faith-building thoughts as opposed to allowing the challenges of a legalistic religion and a poor farm life determine my attitude and future. And I learned that by taking responsibility for my thinking, I could determine the direction of my life. I discovered we can all choose to tell our life story as a victim or as one who has chosen to walk in victory and abundance.

In this very hopeful book, Joel shares his own story of early heartache, tragedy, and misfortune—and how those experiences could have left him trapped in anger, fear, and depression. His continued search for answers and solutions led to his discovery that he was not trapped—he had a choice. He could move beyond those negative emotions to be more empathetic and joyous than ever before. Along the way he learned the fallacy of some common assumptions:

- If I were just able to meet enough people, someone is bound to come along and save me.

- If I can just get a college degree, it will automatically lead to a fulfilling life.

- Location and luck determine my success.

We all dream of and wish for lives of happiness, meaning, and fulfillment. And yet, it seems reality assures us we will experience hardships along the way. We are apparently designed to grow from the unexpected struggles that inevitably show up. But like the butterfly struggling to get out of the cocoon, our struggles are part of what makes us fully alive. And like the butterfly, those struggles are not intended to limit or cripple us, but to allow us to develop our resilience, fortitude, compassion, and personal excellence.

In the award-winning movie *The King's Speech*, circumstances thrust the Duke of York into the role of King George IV. He was challenged to "have faith in his voice" while dealing with a debilitating stammer. That faith was about much more than just pushing words out of his mouth. To find his voice, he had to believe he possessed a message worth sharing. In that gut-wrenching but thrilling process, the duke found his voice, thus becoming confident and able to galvanize his countrymen for uncommon greatness.

Joel describes the process by which we can all make the choices for finding our unique voice—even when circumstances seem to make us stammer. *Finding Your Voice* gently guides us through the process of opening up after being wounded, of trusting after trust has been violated, of stretching in areas that culture and tradition have warned us against, and of acting in our passion even when others say that it's unrealistic and impractical. Joel helps us understand what Maya Angelo meant in saying, "When you know better, you do better." This is a book to help us know, and do, better. Forgiveness, peace, hope, and compassion are characteristics that can be learned. Those healthy traits may not seem natural in light of real-life circumstances, but they can be learned in spite of those circumstances.

I challenge you to open your heart and discover how the unexplained and often unwelcome events in our lives can move us toward the greatness intended for each of us. As we move away from our own hurts and fears, we release the best in ourselves and encourage the same in those around us.

You are doing something special for others and yourself by reading *Finding Your Voice*! The investment of your time will come back multiplied with more confidence and enthusiasm—and you'll discover a powerful voice that will inspire and encourage others along the way.

DAN MILLER
Author and Life Coach
48Days.com

INTRODUCTION

Listen to your voice. No one else can hear it.

Tell your story. No one else can speak it.

Run after your passion. No one else can catch it.

Being true to the person you were created to be is the best
gift you can give yourself, your family, and the world.

A fake voice, whether from a "frienemy" or in a political debate, is easy to identify and difficult to listen to for any length of time. Falseness grates on the nerves and wears on the soul. We *crave* authenticity.

So many people today—maybe even you—struggle through life weighed down by all the people standing on their shoulders: the perfect parent, the fearless leader, the high-achieving employee, the responsible child, the amazing spouse, the caring volunteer, the conscientious money manager. All those voices whisper in your ears like the angel and devil from old cartoons—the angel perched on one shoulder, the devil anchored on the other. They tell you what to say, what to think, what to dream, and how to act. They drown out your authentic voice. Worse, the cacophony of demands and expectations crushes your spirit and keeps you from seeing, thinking, dreaming, and being the person you were designed to be. It's no surprise you've lost your voice—it's a wonder you can even breathe!

Now let me ask you this: Would it be OK for life to go on like this forever—with these characters and their persuasive yet counterfeit voices permanently weighing you down? Do you want to continue shouting against the crowd of voices until you can hardly speak? Since you picked up this book, my guess is that your answer is *no*. I'm willing to bet you want something different—something *better*—for your life. Amid all the noise and confusion and demands, you want to find your voice and experience a life authentic to you.

In *For Love of the Game,* Kevin Costner's character, baseball pitcher Billy Chapel, uses the phrase "clear the mechanism" to get in "the zone." With those words, the outside noises—his teammates' banter, jeers from the opposing team's dugout, the crowd in the stands—all fade into silence. Suddenly, he's able to focus on who he is and what he does best. That's *his* voice.

Here's the good news: like Chapel, your voice is within you. With focus and intention, you can block out the noise and distractions and reconnect with it. When you hear it, there will be no mistaking its authenticity. You won't have to wonder what you're supposed to be doing with your life; you'll *know* without doubt or reservation. And just as important, you'll know what you shouldn't be doing and whom you should ignore. One by one, you can flick those characters off your shoulders until you hear only the voice that really matters—*yours.* Imagine the peace that kind of clarity could bring to your personal and professional life.

YOUR FRIEND IN THE PROCESS

As a life coach, I help people find their voice—not the sound that comes out of one's mouth, but the truth that comes from the soul. You might think of me as the go-to guy for clarity, confidence, and direction. I'm the guy people call when they feel stuck, under-challenged, or overwhelmed. I teach people how to get in touch with who they really are, what excites them, and what they stand for, even if they have no idea where to begin looking.

> ## Questions for Reflection
>
> Within each chapter I've included several *Questions for Reflection*. To get the most out of the *Finding Your Voice* process, it is imperative that you are honest with yourself. Don't simply jot down the "right" answers (i.e., the answers that would please or impress others). Give yourself permission to fully express yourself. It may seem scary at first to admit what you *really* think, but you'll find that *when you tell yourself the truth, fear disappears.*
>
> I encourage you to write your answers in your *Finding Your Voice Journal.* (available for download at FYVBook.com). Additionally, check out the *Finding Your Voice* community online where you can join discussions about the questions and concepts in this book. Go to FYVBook.com to find all of the bonus resources mentioned in this book.

During the past six years, I've worked with clients from the East Coast to the West Coast. Some people come to me because they are in a life transition: a child leaving the nest, a layoff, a divorce, a marriage. Some are dissatisfied in their work. Others know they want something different for their lives but are unclear on what that means or how to go about discovering what that "something" is. Some struggle with the concept of work-life balance. Whatever their initial reason for seeking out a coach and ultimately hiring me, I've learned that most people's needs run deeper than simply navigating the life changes they're facing. What most people really want is clarity about their purpose. They want hope that "this" isn't all there is to life. They want healing from past hurts, trauma, and drama. And they want the confidence to be the most authentic version of themselves. In every case, finding their true voice empowers them to take their life in the direction that best suits them and their personality.

In this book, you'll read stories from several of my clients and friends who have gone through the life-changing journey of finding their voice. These are real people who, perhaps like you, wanted to live a more meaningful, purpose-filled life. With that hope, they began the process of getting back to their true selves. By trusting in themselves and God, they took steps to better understand who they are, to say *yes* to the activities and people that bring them joy, and to change what wasn't working in their lives. Their results vary—which is appropriate since each person is unique. Regardless of where their different journeys took (or are taking) them, one fact remains: they are happier and more fulfilled for having found, listened to, and *embraced* their voice.

Knowing your authentic voice allows you to experience the life you desire at home and in your work. Voice comes from the Latin root *vocare*, which is also the root word for vocation. One of the many ways you can express your voice is through your work—because that's where you spend the most time. But as you read this book, I hope you'll see that *Finding Your Voice* is about so much more than a career choice. It's about giving *full expression* to your true self—holding nothing back.

My job as your coach is to guide you through the process I've seen work in my own life and in the lives of many others. One of the things I'm known for is asking probing questions. (You'll find a lot of them throughout this book.) My clients will tell you I don't give the answers. Why not? I believe each person needs to discover his or her own truth. If I tell you what I think you should do, I become just another voice weighing on your shoulder. No one needs that. Finding your voice isn't pass or fail; it's a progressive process. You will not receive a grade from me for any of the work you do or don't do. You don't have to believe what I believe. This is about you discovering *you*. It's about finding a way back to yourself and reconnecting with your spirit and soul.

My role here is to be your friend in this journey. Not a friend who smiles and nods at everything you say, but a friend who challenges you to find the truth. You know the difference, right? Some people allow their friends to wallow in self-pity or to believe the lies they tell themselves.

That's not me. I'm going to poke you in the ribs when you try to wallow or wiggle your way out of answering tough questions. And those lies you're tempted to believe? Those could just be the beliefs you've come to accept about your value, worth, and potential—beliefs that may have served you for a time in your life but now may be limiting your growth and development. Later in this book, as you examine your own beliefs, you may be surprised to realize how some of them may have kept you locked in place—for years. Disempowering beliefs and lies keep you trapped; it is the truth that will set you free.

The lies you tell yourself keep you trapped; the truth sets you free.

DISCOVERING MY OWN VOICE

I know from personal experience that the ideas outlined in this book work. I have helped people from all walks of life find their voice through my coaching program. But before I could do that, I had to find my own voice—my own passion, purpose, talents, and enduring qualities. My childhood was filled with challenges, physical trauma, and some pretty intense drama that created self-doubt and confusion about who I was and what I could accomplish. I'll share my story in more detail later, but here's the nutshell version.

I almost died when I was five years old. The accident I suffered caused traumatic injuries, but the healing was as much emotional and spiritual as it was physical. My parents had separated a few years before the accident, and each suffered through a journey of guilt, growth, and forgiveness. As an only child, I had a front row seat to their self-destructive behaviors of promiscuous sex, alcohol and drug use, and in my mom's case, an abusive relationship from which it took years for her to untangle. It doesn't take a psychologist (although saw more than one) to explain why

I fought almost daily at school, smoked marijuana and drank as a teen, and engaged in my own risky behaviors as a young adult.

After high school I was extremely disappointed when I couldn't get into the Marines because of the permanent hearing loss caused by my childhood accident. So I did what so many people do when they don't know what they want to be when they grow up: I went to college and majored in general studies. Yep. *General*. Nothing very passionate about that, is there? Later, I put myself through grad school twice, earning an MBA and a master's in counseling. Still, I was uncertain about how to *express* myself—how to share my voice and what I thought I had to offer with the world.

Over and over again, I tried to do the "right" thing by taking traditional, corporate jobs. I enjoyed some successes, but I didn't find fulfillment. And several times I met with all-out failure. Then again, maybe I didn't actually fail. Bestselling author and speaker Robert Allen says, "There is no failure. Only feedback." I think there's something to that. Sure, it feels like failure when you do your best in a given situation and it isn't good enough. But when you consider all you learn in the process, the reality is that you are better for having tried. Like Thomas Edison, who said he hadn't failed 10,000 times at making a light bulb but had found 10,000 ways that didn't work, when you try something that doesn't work, you discover information—feedback—that helps you grow.

Looking back, I can see how each of my experiences revealed clues that helped me discover my voice. Those clues acted as signposts pointing me to the career and life I enjoy today. My trauma- and drama-filled history planted seeds of excitement for helping people find their voice. For example, I can remember one time very clearly when my mom's boyfriend charged at me when I was just ten. My mom did what any mom would do; she came to my rescue and unapologetically took a stand for me. Her unselfish act sent a shockwave through my system. Although I wasn't able to process and understand what it meant at the time, it triggered a desire in me to do the same—to be one who stands in the gap for women everywhere. Today, I know I'm doing what I was created to do.

GET INTENTIONAL ABOUT YOUR JOURNEY

My inclination was to title this section: Your Journey Begins Now. But really, that's not true. Your journey began the day you were born. With your commitment to finding your voice, today is the day you get intentional. This adventure begins by taking an unflinching look at your life, which isn't always easy. In fact, it can be downright depressing, even painful, to be completely honest with yourself. But when you block out the hard parts or try to forget failed ventures and false starts, you miss feedback that could help you grow and learn. Once you understand how past events shaped your life, you can begin the self-recovery process of reclaiming your authentic voice.

Did you notice I called this a self-*recovery* rather than a self-*discovery* process? Now, don't panic, *Finding Your Voice* isn't a twelve-step program—although many people find healing along the way. One of the goals of this journey is to recover the energy, excitement, and mojo you lost somewhere in the hustle and bustle and ups and downs of your occasionally (or perpetually) chaotic life. (And, of course, you'll *discover* some things as well.) You see, the entire spectrum of our life experiences—the good, the bad, the ugly, and even the very ugly—blend together to create

⚠ **Safety Steps**

Throughout this book you'll see the *Safety Steps* icon followed by a question or suggested activity. When you see one, I encourage you to immediately do the activity or answer the question in your *Finding Your Voice Journal*.

As you take Safety Steps, share your progress with our online community at FYVBook.com. Let us cheer you on!

the light we need to see the next step, and the next, until we get where it is we really want to be.

The blessing is that when you refresh your perspective, you find hope. Hope is an exciting and powerful emotion that opens the door to amazing possibilities. As you work through the content and exercises in this book, you'll learn how to harness hope as well as other emotions that may be nudging you to change. You'll acquire a deeper, richer understanding of your abilities and strengths. Understanding yourself at a deeper level will help you define who you really are. And, ultimately, my goal is for you find the confidence to move forward and fully experience and express the voice placed within you.

You may feel as if you've lost your voice—that you are not the person you used to be, or the person you want to be. *Finding Your Voice* will help you find your way back. Let's get started.

Chapter One

GRASPING FOR HOPE

I stood by, waiting for the "go" sign. The scene had become an all-too-common ritual. My mom's boyfriend, Doyle, rank with alcohol and high on whatever he could buy on the way home from work (cocaine, usually), came crashing into her house. Of course he lived there, too, but on payday Friday, neither of us wanted him around. He shouted obscenities and stormed around the house in wild fury. He wanted to intimidate my mom physically and emotionally—but Mom didn't make that easy.

The first few times I witnessed Doyle's outbursts, they terrified me. But now, as much as I hated it, the ugliness seemed almost predictable. The abuse had been going on for years. And drugs...they were just part of his everyday life. I lost count of the number of times I watched him snort coke or smoke weed. But watching him threaten my mom was another story; for this, I hated him.

Here we go again, I thought as I ducked out of his path. At ten years old, I wasn't big enough to hold him off. Besides, I'd long since learned that speaking up or jumping between Doyle and Mom only made him angrier and meaner. Instead, I watched for Mom's signal to run for help if things got "bad enough." The shouting and shoving went both ways. Mom was feisty and didn't stand for being threatened. I remember the strength in her voice as she told him to get out the house. "You're drunk, you're high—if I can't make you leave, I'll get someone who can!" Finally, she nodded at me and I dashed out the door.

Damp with sweat, my T-shirt clung to my pudgy tween-age body. Rocks and broken glass poked my feet as I ran barefoot to the pay phone at the convenience store down the block. Still gasping to catch my breath, I grabbed the receiver and pushed "0."

A far-away voice came on the line. "Operator."

"We need the police," I said working to sound grown up and in control. My mom needed a hero and if I couldn't fight off Doyle myself, I was determined to get someone who could.

"If this is an emergency, son, you need to call 9-1-1," the operator replied. "I'll put you through, but next time you need to dial 9-1-1. Do you understand?"

I nodded into the phone. A few clicks later the police dispatcher came on the line.

"What is your emergency?"

I had made the run before, so it felt almost routine to repeat the words: "We need the police. We need them to come to my house," I said. "My mom's boyfriend is trying to hurt her. We need help—*now.*" *Just come get him; take the jerk away,* I thought.

After giving the dispatcher our address, I hung up and raced back to the house. I breathed a sigh of relief when the police cruiser pulled onto my street. Like an air traffic controller, I waved the officers toward my mom's house.

I'm sure at that point they told me to stay outside. I really can't remember. But I do remember them taking Doyle away.

Back inside, I helped my mom clean up pieces of broken glass and to set the house back in order. As odd as it may seem, Doyle's episode didn't ruin our evening. After picking up, we went back to life as usual. I know now that Mom's cool, collected behavior and determined spirit taught me some expert (but not necessarily healthy) coping skills. We didn't discuss the ugliness; we just moved on.

As bad as those years of watching my mom's abuser create chaos and confusion in our lives were, that's not where my story really begins...

BROKEN BODY, BROKEN FAMILY

The chain of events that led to the "payday Friday" ritual began, for me, when my parents divorced. I was three when they separated and don't really remember the divorce itself, except for impressions of sadness that we were no longer all together. I have a huge memory gap for that period of time, not because I was too young, but because of what happened next.

One Sunday when I was five, I went on a hike with my dad, one of his friends, and a couple other kids. After a while, we came to a wide, dry creek bed with a train trestle crossing over it. Dad and his friend set us loose to play while they rested. For an adventurous and precocious five-year-old boy and his friends, the trestle looked like a jungle gym. It didn't take long for one of us to come up with the bright idea of climbing up the side of the ravine to the bridge above while the adults' heads were turned. At the top, we tested our balance and independence by lying down on the railroad ties and peeking out over the edge. Full of pride, we shouted a happy "Hi!" to my Dad and his friend below.

You can guess their reaction. They jumped up and yelled for us to get down as they immediately began climbing the ravine wall to fetch us. Halfway up, Dad heard the horn sound in the distance. I was so busy playing I didn't notice the train until it was almost on top of me. The noise and vibration startled me, and I fell thirty feet, landing hard on the parched earth below.

By the time Dad reached the top, the train had screeched to a halt and I had disappeared from the bridge. A passenger standing between the cars of the idling train pointed to the creek bed and shouted, "Someone's down there!" Dad raced back down and found me lying on my side in a pool of blood. Fearing I was dead, he knelt down and felt for a pulse. With great relief, he discovered my little heart was still pumping—barely.

These were the days before everyone had cell phones, so one of the train's engineers called for an ambulance. I'd lost so much blood by the time the ambulance arrived, my veins had collapsed and the EMT couldn't start an IV. At the hospital, a team of doctors went to work on me. They discovered three skull fractures, one of which punctured my right middle ear. Several hours of surgery later, my parents were told to expect the worst. Doctors predicted I would die. If I was lucky enough to live, they were certain I would have extensive brain damage.

Can you imagine what life must have been like for my family while I lay there in the hospital? My recently divorced parents were in that all too common transition back to the single life. Their marital relationship was in ruins, their faith sorely tested, and their only child lay broken before them with bleak prospects for recovery. Beneath the terror of not knowing whether I would survive, hovered the fear of what I would be like if I ever woke up. Would I be able to walk or talk? Would I experience any permanent mental, emotional, or physical damage?

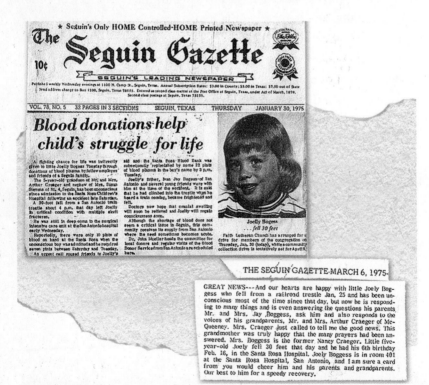

A thirty-foot fall left me in critical condition with multiple skull fractures. My grandparents' community offered life-saving support through blood donations.

My dad describes this time as the "most awful, horrible, guilt-ridden time" of his life. A few days before the accident, he had been hired to start a new job as an editor with Southwest Research Institute. He reported to his first day on the job the day after the accident. For weeks, he went to work every day, not knowing if his son would ever come out of that coma.

Mom was working through nursing school and struggling to make ends meet. We'd been living with her sister until just before the accident. We survived on food stamps and $100 a month from her aunt. The accident occurred during her finals, so, like my dad, she couldn't stay at the hospital; doing so have required her to drop out and restart the program. Thankfully, her classmates voted to allow her special conditions—more written reports in lieu of some of the in-person practicums—so she could make the trek from her home in Austin to the hospital in San Antonio, Texas.

The doctors' prognosis: Don't expect Joel to lead a normal life. They were sure right about that.

I can only imagine how desperate, stressed out, and helpless my parents must have felt as they waited for me to wake. After three long weeks, I shocked everyone by finally coming out the coma. But even after I revived, I had a lot of healing to do. I was incredibly weak on my right side and had to regain the strength to walk. Temporary paralysis gave me a limp—not unlike trying to walk after your leg has fallen asleep. Adding to that was the injury to my right ear, which caused permanent hearing loss on that side and threw off my sense of balance. My eyesight was also affected. Doctors assured my parents I had suffered permanent brain damage. Their prognosis: Don't expect Joel to lead a normal life.

They were sure right about that.

FROM BAD TO WORSE

The accident left long-term scars on everyone in my family. I stayed in the hospital for another month, but regaining my balance and learning to cope with the hearing loss took significantly longer. As devastating as those wounds were, they only account for my physical challenges. Mentally and emotionally, we each had bigger battles to fight.

Before I get any further into this story, I want to interject an important comment: I don't place judgment or blame on my family for the things you will read here. Everyone approaches life from a unique set of experiences and knowledge. Our perspective of the world, our relationships, and our own abilities develop as a result of the experiences and the information we gather on our life's journey. Our expectations for success or failure come from that perspective. As we learn and grow, our perspective and behaviors change. That certainly happened in my life and in my parents' lives. I hope the same thing happens for you as you find your voice.

"We do the best we can with what we know, and when we know better, we do better." —Maya Angelou

Feelings of guilt about the accident crushed Dad's spirit for years. Drinking and sex were his vices. Going to bars and picking up women became a regular pastime—one I joined him in far too early in life. By the time I reached middle school, I was an accomplished wingman and knew how to order my dad's Martell on the rocks at the bar. I remember one night when the car ride on the way home from our evenings out turned into an adventure as we veered this way and that to miss oncoming traffic. Dad lost control of the pink Ford Thunderbird he drove. Of course, there were no seat belt laws at the time. I tried desperately and unsuccessfully to hold onto the seat, the doorframe, anything to keep from flying around the car as it skidded off the road. Finally, the car landed hard in a ditch. Shaken but unharmed, Dad put the car back in gear and managed to get us home.

My mom faced demons of a different sort. Her boyfriend, Doyle, moved in with her shortly after the accident. He was a user and abuser in every sense of the word. I lived with my dad but visited Mom every other weekend. I hated the nights when Doyle came home drunk and high after hanging out with his friends. Mom tried to protect me from the brunt of the ugliness. She locked the doors and told him to go sleep it off and leave us alone. But if you know any "mean drunks," you know just telling them to leave isn't very effective. Instead, he pounded on the door while yelling obscenities. I remember once he threw his body against the door so forcefully that the molding on the frame cracked. Sometimes he kept enough wits about him to break the glass window on the kitchen door so he could simply reach through, turn the lock, and let himself in the house.

And then there were the parties. This was Austin, Texas, in the late 1970s and early 1980s. Drugs were part of the scene. Doyle and his brothers hosted parties for their friends, and I saw plenty of marijuana joints and trays of cocaine. (Once, I remember feeling simultaneously impressed and disgusted as I watched someone snort cocaine through a rolled up $100 bill.) Mom attempted to keep me away from the worst of it—generally making sure I stayed out of the room where the "festivities" were taking place. At one party though, Doyle handed a tray with lines of coke to his brother who was standing a few steps behind and off to the side of me. I'd been attending their parties since I was a little kid so the drug scene felt fairly normal—or at least not out of the ordinary. But I knew that cocaine was different, more dangerous, and I *knew* he shouldn't be flaunting it like that around me. I found my mom in another room and told her what had happened. Man, she hit the roof! After she told Doyle off, we left the party. He ran out into the parking lot and begged her to stay. Not a chance. For all the crap she endured from that man, her mama bear instincts showed up in a big way when she felt I was being put in harm's way.

As I witnessed my parents' destructive behaviors, I picked up unhealthy habits for dealing with my own challenges. With my balance issues, I became the kid who was *picked last* for sports, but *picked on* most. I could lie and say the teasing didn't bother me, but detailed records from school administrators tell the truth. Once I regained my strength, I developed quite a reputation as a fighter. I lost count of the number of times my dad left work to retrieve me from the principal's office. Kids teased me for the way I walked and talked, and I let them have it. In my dad's words, I "would get on top of them and pound the hell out of them." After a while, I didn't just retaliate, I *looked* for the opportunity to fight. Proving, with my fists, that I was just as good as everyone else was my way of seeking acceptance and significance.

FINDING HOPE

Looking back, it's easy to think *our lives were a mess!* But in those moments, I now know we were all doing our best to deal with life the only way we knew how. We each coped with our emotions, weaknesses, and needs differently. For all the hardship and struggle we endured and put ourselves through, I can also look back now and see we were grasping for hope.

Hope. It's a short word that exudes enormous possibilities. Hope is the reason people pick up a book, hire a coach, apply for a new job, go back to school, open a business, or set off on a trip around the world. The faintest glimmer of hope may be all you need to see your way to the first steps in your path of development.

When weather forecasters predict a big storm, one of the first things people do is go out and buy batteries for their flashlights. Why? Simple. We know that when the power goes out, even the tiny beam of a flashlight can enable us to see. When the storms of life hit, we instinctively reach for hope. And if the beam of light seems narrow and dim, you can recharge hope by getting a new perspective on your life and the way you fit into this world.

For me, that "recharge" began just before middle school. My parents recognized my interest in martial arts and signed me up for classes. If you haven't studied martial arts, old Kung Fu movies or scenes from *The Karate Kid* may have given you the wrong impression. If you are a serious student, the benefits run much deeper than winning competitions. I discovered a love for martial arts and learned a great deal about determination and persistence.

Later, at age seventeen, I began to study Tae Kwon Do. I spent many an afternoon practicing at the dojo. The master and his sons became like a second family as they mentored me in the mechanics and the meaning of the sport. The tenets of Tae Kwon Do are courtesy, integrity, perseverance, self-control, and indomitable spirit. Wow, did I need those things in my life! Don't we all? Focusing on those characteristics daily allowed them to sink into my spirit and eventually become part of me.

The self-discipline I developed while studying martial arts renewed some of the confidence I lost after the accident. Things weren't all rosy from that point on, but my practice shaped my character in a powerful way. My impaired sense of balance required me to work harder than the average student. The fact that the doctors said I couldn't do what other kids my age were capable of spurred me to prove them wrong. In my mind, their prognosis was unacceptable. Pei, my beautiful wife, once told me, "You know, honey, I think those doctors did you a favor by telling you what you 'couldn't' do." She's right. Proving them wrong became a powerful motivator for me. So much so, I eventually earned my black belt and went on to train other students. And like those who mentored me, my role wasn't simply teaching people the mechanics of a punching or kicking motion. The real lessons were about self-confidence, overcoming challenges, and finding inner strength—something I'm still privileged to do every day. I didn't know it back then, but helping others grow was a step toward finding my voice.

Questions for Reflection

- What have you learned from past events (good or bad) about your resiliency?

- What habits or routines have you developed to help you cope with challenges or difficult circumstances? Are those habits or routines helping or harming you?

- We've all been disappointed before—by leaders, by close relationships, and events or situations. Are you willing to pick yourself up, dust off, and try again?

CHAPTER SUMMARY

What statement or story from this chapter resonated with you the most? Why?

_____

_____

_____

_____

_____

_____

_____

_____

How could this help you find *your* voice?

_____

_____

_____

_____

_____

_____

_____

_____

_____

Chapter Two

DO YOU KNOW YOUR OWN VOICE?

What does it mean to "find your voice"?

- It means getting in touch with your emotions and what excites you.

- It means understanding your value and worth.

- It means knowing the *real* you.

- It is *your* full expression.

Your voice affects everything you do. When it's clear and strong, you feel strong; you are also at peace with your choices because you live with intention. When you know your voice, you don't need someone else to give you approval because you've already approved of yourself.

In the previous chapter I mentioned that I started to hear my voice when I began helping people overcome challenges and draw on their inner strength. But even in my own journey, finding my voice wasn't an overnight experience. I hit roadblock after roadblock as I sought significance through others' approval. Ultimately, I discovered that until you know and embrace who you are, it's impossible to be fully in harmony with yourself.

KNOWING YOUR VOICE

Finding Your Voice isn't a process you can move through in a neat, sequential order. It isn't a cookie-cutter program, because, after all, you are not a cookie. You are a unique and amazing individual with the power to create the life you desire. The tools and suggestions I'll share in *Finding Your Voice* will guide you through a personal journey that is more art than science. I encourage you to try out these tools and see which ones work for you. If a strategy strikes a chord with you, use it! If one of the tools doesn't feel like a fit, that's OK too. The point is: this isn't a rule-book, it's a guide that will help you find or get reacquainted with your voice.

Rediscovering the real you will change the way you approach life and the opportunities and challenges it presents. Once you know your voice—once you know who you are, what you stand for, and what excites you—it will become easier to decide what you want to take on and what you want to let go.

Before we get into the *how* of finding your voice, let's take a look at what your voice encompasses. When you know your voice, you:

- *Value* your enduring qualities and unique traits,
- *Own* who you are and understand what is important to you,
- Are *intentional* with your thoughts and actions,
- *Create* a plan by visualizing your best life,
- And *embrace* your excitement and emotions.

Let me take a moment to expand on each of these statements.

VOICE

Knowing your voice means *valuing your enduring qualities and unique traits.* When you see your innate value—and yes, *you are valuable*—a light begins to shine within you. Rather than hiding in the shadows, tuning into your voice empowers you to see ways that you can: 1) make your corner of the world a brighter, more vibrant, and exciting place, and 2) go out into the world and let your light—your gifts, experiences, knowledge, compassion, and skills—shine on others. The world, your family, your friends and coworkers, the people at church, and those in your community need you to find your voice so they can experience you at your finest. They also need you to find your voice so you can help them find theirs.

> *Your success and well-being isn't only about you. When you thrive, you encourage and inspire others.*

Let me share one quick testimonial from the daughter of one of my clients, Kim, who you'll read about in Chapter Four. Kim approached the coaching process very intentionally. She participated fully and completed her homework thoroughly and thoughtfully. As a result, she came away with a solid plan of action to help make her voice sing. I interviewed one of her daughters, Alexis, on my podcast to get her take on the differences she'd seen in her mom's life and, by extension, in their family's life. She first spoke of the happiness and excitement she hears in her mom's voice as they talk almost daily on the phone. That audible joy is a big change from the despondency Kim expressed before we began working together. That positive shift in and of itself is awesome, but I love what Alexis said next: "I think her going through this process jump-started all of us. It's been exciting! My mom and my sister and I have started an accountability group—a place where we can check in once a week to talk about our goals—Have we made progress? What are we struggling with?—and what we want to celebrate with each other." The three women in this family all have entrepreneurial aspirations. Because Kim acted with courage and put her dreams in motion, her daughters are following suit by pursuing their own dreams. To me, *that's exciting*! Your success and well-being isn't only about you. When you thrive, you encourage and inspire others.

It feels amazing to know who you are and to stop trying to be someone you're not. But the personal benefits aren't even the best part. Think about it: Who else benefits when you are at your best? Everyone, right? When you use your unique gifts and do what you love, you exude energy; happiness pours out of you and covers the people around you.

VOICE

Knowing your voice means *owning who you are and understanding what is important to you.* Who are you really? When you look in the mirror, do you feel as if you're looking at a stranger or do you feel you know yourself pretty well? Another way to approach this question is to think about how we develop over time. One of the first questions I ask my clients is: "As people grow in age, wisdom, and maturity, do we become different people, or do we grow more into our own skin?" The responses I get usually make for good, back-and-forth discussion and bring up new ideas for consideration. One of those ideas is the belief that, over time, we tend to become more of who we are—who we were created to be. That concept can be freeing and downright empowering.

In *Strength Finders 2.0*, author Tom Rath says his research indicates that most people tend to become more themselves as they grow. And why not? You were made with a unique personality. How would it feel to have the freedom to be fully yourself? When you find your voice, you will *experience* that freedom. This journey will also reveal what, if anything, may be preventing you from expressing your true self so you can remove the invisible chains that have held you captive.

VOICE

Knowing your voice means *being intentional.* The way you do anything is the way you do everything. It's unreasonable to expect a rich, rewarding life if you approach things haphazardly. Being intentional requires you to choose your thoughts, words, and actions, knowing that how you live today affects the outcomes you experience tomorrow.

Making the commitment to live intentionally and authentically allows you to filter out others' messages, rules, and beliefs when they don't apply to you. It also frees you to focus your time, resources, and talent on the people and projects you care about the most. What would your life be like if you devoted the best of yourself to what really matters? How would those people and projects benefit? Like a laser beam engraves a precise message on a piece of jewelry, your focused attention can leave a beautiful mark on your life and on the lives of those you love.

> Be careful of your thoughts, for your thoughts become your words.
> Be careful of your words, for your words become your actions.
> Be careful of your actions, for your actions become your habits.
> Be careful of your habits, for your habits become your character.
> Be careful of your character, for your character becomes your destiny.
> —Author unknown

VOICE

Finding your voice means *creating a life plan by visualizing your best life*. Dave Ramsey, author of the bestselling book *The Total Money Makeover*, takes a counterintuitive approach to a truism many of us are familiar with: Without a clear vision, people perish. He says the idea isn't about *vision* per se, but about how to *perish*. The lesson Dave is trying to communicate is - if you want to know how to perish, it's simple: live without vision. Unfortunately, that's how most people live their lives. Without vision or a plan, they take whatever life hands them—which generally isn't much.

In contrast, those who make time to create a vision and plan for their lives often receive more wealth, greater pleasure, and better relationships than they have ever imagined. Beyond the success, because vision creates enthusiasm, they have more fun experiencing life.

Your vision is like a highlight reel of possibilities. Over and over again, I've watched people who took the time to develop a picture of what they want, become almost giddy at the prospect of seeing their vision come to fruition. For example, my client Carolyn used the Vision Board Activity in Chapter Six to paint a picture of a life infused with her love for dance—something she was thrilled to rediscover in herself. Jeff, another client, set his inner child free to enjoy the process of creating a Vision Board and says: "My Vision Board hangs in my home office. I look at it daily. The inspiration and passion are what get me up in the morning. I love it." And my client Colleen says, "Having done a Vision Board just a few months ago, the words still elicit the positive and strong emotions that I experienced when I made it. I can quickly look at the board to see what I've achieved and get visual reminders of what is yet to come."

You can see examples of Carolyn, Jeff, and Colleen's Vision Boards (along with many others) at FYVBook.com.

Without a vision or a plan, you are destined to play out a dream that might belong to someone else, but not to you. I strongly encourage you to go all out when you create your vision for your life. Have fun with the process and use your imagination!

VOICE

Finding your voice means *embracing and harnessing your emotions.* *Harness* is a word I use frequently in the coaching sessions. It is an encouragement for my clients to allow the force and power of the emotion they're experiencing to pull them forward in their journey. Too often, the only emotion we allow ourselves to heed is fear. But I believe emotions can be promptings that, if harnessed, can lead to a fuller and more enriching life.

Consider how you would feel if you did more of what brings you joy. The answer is obvious, right? You would feel *more joyful*. Finding your voice is about letting the excitement of your full emotional potential carry you forward.

HOW DID YOU LOSE YOUR VOICE IN THE FIRST PLACE?

It seems impossible that we could ever lose touch with our soul's voice. I mean, it's part of who we are, right? And yet, I've worked with people from all ages and career paths who struggle to hear and heed their own voices. In Chapter Five, I'll out a few culprits that may be trying to steal your voice and stifle the real you. But since that's a few chapters away, let's take a look now at one of the most common and unsuspecting reasons people lose their voice: our culture of conformity.

If you followed the traditional track—elementary school, high school, college, day job—you've spent the majority of your life working to please others. In school, teachers penalized you for not knowing the right answers. Your parents probably had their say about any poor grades on your report cards as well. But academics are only part of the issue. Movies about "mean girls," jocks versus nerds, and the conflicts between "greasers" and "socs" exist for a reason. Starting at a very early age, our culture demands conformity. Fitting in is essential for survival. Even "misfits" and rebels create their own social cliques. They want to fight conformity and appear different; eventually they end up looking a lot alike.

After high school and college, the pressure to fit in changes as it intensifies. *The Joneses* with Demi Moore and David Duchovny offered an extreme yet true-to-life example of how social pressure affects our happiness, our relationships, even the way we spend our money. In the movie, Moore and Duchovny play the role of parents in an affluent, happy family. In reality, they are actors. A marketing company supplies them with all the *stuff* that signifies success: fancy cars, designer clothes and accessories, and the perfect house. They're paid to make people want what they have—and it works. Why? Well, think about it. How many people in your neighborhood drive the same make (or comparable) car, wear similar clothing and jewelry styles, watch the same movies, eat at the same restaurants, work traditional office jobs, vote for the same candidates, take annual week-long vacations, and fill-in their off hours with similar hobbies?

We possess an innate need for community. Sometimes it seems the best way to connect with others is to follow the crowd—like what they like, believe what they believe, do what they do, and live how they live.

Don't get me wrong, participating in a healthy community is a good thing. We all need a support network of friends we can count on and who can rely on us. Community is an important part of being human. But unlike a sorority, fraternity, or the golf club, your personal community—the people you spend time with and value most—shouldn't require you to pay "sameness" dues. And yet, many people pay those dues every day. How? They spend money they don't have on things they don't want to impress people who may not even notice. In the end, they're in debt and exhausted from pretending to care about things that just don't matter to them. Worse, they're no closer to developing real relationships than when they started. What they don't realize—and what I hope you're starting to get—is that community doesn't necessitate uniformity. You can be part of a vibrant community and still be uniquely you.

Let me add a side note here and say that the activities you choose to participate in to fulfill your need for camaraderie may be socially acceptable or even considered commendable. Even so, they can still be draining if they don't support and uplift the real you. For example, "Nicolette" recently left a leadership role at Celebrate Recovery. The internationally respected organization serves a worthy and important need by helping people overcome addictions. However, after evaluating her purpose, vision, and goals for the season of life she is in, she chose to step down from her responsibility. Although Nicolette appreciates the mission of the organization, being personally involved at such an intense level robbed her of the time and energy she needed to fulfill her dreams. It wasn't an easy decision, but it was the right one for her. "With every passing day, the peace I feel inside increases and confirms the decision," she told me a few weeks after resigning.

Peace is a good measuring stick. When you consider agreeing to participate in an activity, take a job, or make a major purchase, ask yourself: "Do I feel at peace about adding this activity or responsibility to my life? Does this support me in being true to myself and my current goals?" If the answer is a clear yes, then go for it! If something twists inside you and makes you uneasy with the decision, you may want to respond by saying, "Maybe next time. Right now isn't good for me." Refuse to allow the culture of conformity to decide your fate.

WHY IS IT IMPORTANT TO FIND YOUR VOICE?

If conformity feels natural, why is it necessary to find your authentic voice? Couldn't you be happy just going with the flow? I bet you know the answer. Even if you don't know how to put it into words yet, you can *feel* it.

Following the crowd (consciously or unconsciously) can become a habit. Since you picked up this book, my guess is that habit no longer serves you. Maybe it's the sick feeling in the pit of your stomach or the pounding in your chest you experience on the way to work. Or maybe it's the jolt of excitement you experience when you allow yourself to imagine something more, different, or better, than the life you're living now. Those feelings—or symptoms—are your heart and soul's way of trying to get your attention. I hope your symptoms are past the point of mild discomfort. I hope subsisting within the status quo is actually causing you at least a little "pain." Not because I want you to suffer—of course not! But through years of coaching, I've learned that when the pain of staying the same exceeds the pain of growth and fear of change, *that's* the turning point. That's when you have not only the desire, but also the determination to take a chance on finding a way back to yourself. My friend Larry Winget, The Pitbull of Personal Development®, explains that the only way to get to a better place is to get so upset and disgusted with your present situation, staying where you are is no longer an option.

WHY DOES IT TAKE SO LONG?

A woman recently asked, "Why did it take me so long to find my voice?" Perhaps one reason is because, as Larry points out, people generally don't change until they must. For a long time, this woman, who is an amazingly creative photographer, felt lost. Surrounded by people who don't "get" her artistic style, she tried and failed for years to fit in. It killed her spirit to take staged, "smile at the camera" photos. But that's what people pay for, right? Shoot after shoot, she grew more disgusted with the work. Taking pictures, once something she loved, became a chore. Until one day it clicked: she didn't have to squander her talent on those who didn't appreciate it. She took down her website and opened an Instagram account. The calls for mundane jobs stopped, and she rediscovered her love for capturing the beauty of simple moments. Slowly, and only by looking within and being completely honest with herself, has she found her voice, her strengths, her innate worth, and a new, freeing sense of power. And guess what? The world has noticed. Just by being herself and doing what she loves, she has attracted all sorts of amazing opportunities. Suddenly, people from the other side of the globe started contacting her about her work. They're captivated by her style and the way she sees the world.

It took years to permit herself to speak—or in this case take photos—without worrying about others' expectations. Although she's thrilled with

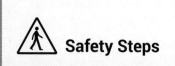

Safety Steps

Identify at least three things you enjoy doing. Schedule time on your calendar to do one of those activities this week.

her new life, she feels frustrated at having lost so much time trying to be someone else. The reality is, time is a key element in the process. Growth requires time and patience. Thankfully, the results are worth the effort.

You're Getting Hotter!

Here's a fun way of thinking about getting closer to or further from your voice. Think about the "hotter, colder" game you may have played with your son or daughter. You hide a surprise, perhaps it's an Easter egg or special present, and then guide your child through the process of finding it by saying, "You're getting warmer," or "You're getting colder." When your child is right on top of the gift you watch with excitement and shout, "You're getting hot! You're on fire!" Gift in hand, your little one's face lights up.

Now think about this: How do *you* feel when you see that look of joy and wonder on your child's face? Life is full of hidden treasures that are just waiting to be discovered. When you hear the voice placed within you shouting "You're getting hot! You're on fire!", just like with your children, your face lights up, and your entire countenance changes. The search isn't designed to frustrate you, but to help you fully appreciate the gifts and treasures you will find.

BE PATIENT WITH YOUR PROGRESS

The life cycle of the giant Chinese bamboo tree illustrates the importance of allowing time for growth. When the farmer plants the bamboo seed, he makes a long-term commitment. He gives the seedling the right amount of water, sunlight, and nourishment, and he waits. During the entire first year, nothing happens. The second year, he continues to water and fertilize, but still nothing yet. Years three and four pass, nothing. Finally, five years after planting the bamboo, the farmer is rewarded for his patience. In a span of six weeks, the tree grows ninety feet.

Imagine what would happen if, discouraged by a lack of visible growth, the farmer abandoned the seedling in the second or third year.

Without water or the proper nourishment, it wouldn't survive. But an experienced farmer knows that even though there is no visible evidence, the plant is growing a strong network of roots. Reaching deep into the soil, these roots are essential to the plant's development. In year five, the root system supports the bamboo as it grows at a rate of almost forty inches a day.

Now suppose that tree grew nearly a hundred feet without a strong root system. You and I both know it wouldn't stand a chance even against the adversity of a mild breeze, let alone a fierce gust of wind or a strong storm. The bamboo needs a solid foundation to stand tall. So do you.

Intimately knowing your voice allows you to stand your ground. When others tell you what they think you *should* do, you won't be easily swayed by their opinions. This strength of character enhances every area of your life—from your relationships, to your career choices, to the way you choose to enjoy your free time. Developing those roots (the real you) enables you to produce fruits (results) with courage and confidence.

The good news is that your voice and all the power it contains is already within you. The challenge is mustering the courage to find and *use it.*

CHAPTER SUMMARY

What statement or story from this chapter resonated with you the most? Why?

_____

_____

_____

_____

_____

_____

_____

_____

How could this help you find _your_ voice?

_____

_____

_____

_____

_____

_____

_____

_____

_____

Chapter Three

WHAT'S YOUR STORY?

Everyone has a story. Maybe your story involves a traumatic event or accident. Or your story might include the drawn-out drama of a strained or abusive relationship or a hurting marriage. Maybe you're facing a financial, career, or health crisis. Or perhaps you are dealing with a challenging child, or are sending your teen out of the nest for the first time.

It's unnecessary to rate our stories and compare our challenges to the hardships of others. The fact of the matter is, whether you're struggling with an immediate crisis or trying to cope with pain from your past, it hurts. Thankfully, hurts are never wasted. In fact, I believe we're allowed to go through challenges so we can learn, grow, and develop from them. It's like we're being put in a furnace. A furnace's tremendous heat makes even the strongest metals bendable and malleable. Whether God caused the circumstance, or simply allowed them to take place, He can use the heat from your challenges to shape your character and your life.

A lot of people feel discomfort in their day-to-day lives. They dislike their job. They are unhappy with their weight or health. They're unfulfilled by the circumstances of their lives. But it isn't until the heat gets turned up that they feel compelled to do anything about their discomfort. I've talked to so many people who are dissatisfied with their lives. Some even say they want coaching—that they want to cut through the clutter and find their voice. But they don't pull the trigger and write the first check or make the first appointment. Why? The excuses vary:

"I don't have any money."

"I've got bills coming up."

"I'm too busy."

But those aren't the real reasons for not hiring a coach and committing to change. When I hear excuses from folks, what they are really saying is, "I can still tolerate this (boss, weight, debt, misery) a little longer."

Remember that it isn't until the pain of staying the same becomes greater than the pain of stepping outside the comfort zone that anyone commits to change.

Are you ready for a change? Are you uncomfortable enough with your present circumstances to do something different?

Would it be OK if your life was the same five years from now?

Do you feel worthy of a better life—of the best life you can possibly have?

Or do you believe you deserve the challenges, pain, and unhappiness you're enduring?

IS YOUR PAST DICTATING YOUR PRESENT?

While the events, trauma, and drama may have shaped your present circumstances and beliefs, they don't have to dictate your future. You don't have to remain chained to your past mistakes or others' perceptions of you.

Many people look at their lives and think, I've screwed things up so completely...I deserve the mess I'm in. Still others believe lies they heard from authority figures and/or the media: You're not good/smart/pretty/sexy/_____ enough to deserve a better life. If thoughts like those threaten to hold you captive in an unhappy or unfulfilling life, know this: Your biography doesn't have to be your destiny. Your past mistakes and even your present circumstances don't define you.

Imagine carrying a fifty-pound rock around with you everywhere you go. Before long, your hands are scraped and your arms burn. You try carrying it in a backpack, but after a while, that weight causes your back and shoulders to ache. Running with the rock is difficult. Swimming? Forget it. Dancing? Well, you look less than graceful with that dead weight dragging you down. Then one day, looking at the heavy rock crushing your lap, you realize *you are the one doing all the work.* The rock offers nothing in return other than a sore back and calloused hands. Beyond the physical pain and exhaustion, you're frustrated by all the things you *can't* do because your hands are occupied and your energy totally consumed. You've carried it around so long you can't even remember why you picked it up in the first place.

Disempowering beliefs from your past are like that fifty-pound rock. Perhaps manageable for a while, but over time can keep you from moving freely and uninhibited. If you've held onto a belief for years, you may not even recall where it came from—it has become a part of you. It may even seem true. Because they may appear to be based in reality, long-held beliefs can warp your view of your worth and abilities. But remember what I said in the Introduction: Lies hold you back; the truth sets you free.

From my own experiences and my clients' successes, I've learned the value of taking the time to evaluate beliefs. In Chapter Five, I've included an exercise that will help you identify words, situations, or events from as far back as childhood that could be weighing you down. When you uncover the source of a belief that has limited your potential and joy, you can decide whether or not it's worth the extra effort to lug it around. Oftentimes, understanding why you have felt incapable of moving forward is in itself curative. With a simple decision, you can choose to lay down a worn-out belief and walk away lighter, happier, and freer.

Other times, making the necessary mental and emotional shift requires more effort—especially if someone has hurt you deeply. The tendency can be to hold on to anger, resentment, or hurt feelings, because it feels as if you're punishing the person who wronged you. But that's like swallowing poison day after day and expecting the other person to get sick. In reality, the individual you're harboring bitterness against probably isn't even aware of your pain. And they certainly won't suffer any ill effects from the corrosive venom you ingest every time you choose to dwell on past events.

So how can you forgive someone who has caused you pain?

Essentially, it's a spiritual choice. I realized not long ago that even though I thought I had moved beyond the events of my past, I still felt hurt, even a little angry, that my mom permitted me to ever be around her abusive boyfriend and other emotionally toxic situations. Years had passed and the fact that she had allowed me to witness her nightmare and even take part in some of the drug and alcohol use still bothered me.

(Please understand that I'm not picking on my mom here. My dad put me in similar circumstances at bars, other people's houses, and even in our own home. However, our relationship was much more open through the years, and we dealt with any confusing or hurt feelings years ago.)

While preparing the content for this book, I took a hard look at my relationship with my mom and realized that even though significant healing had occurred in both our lives, I still carried around past hurts. Rather than moving on, I paid a lot of unhealthy attention to the hurt that churned inside me. Like that fifty-pound rock, a spirit of unforgiveness weighed heavily on our relationship. An honest evaluation of my heart and actions revealed the truth: It was unfair to judge her past behavior by my current standards.

Intellectually, I knew we all do the best we can with what we know at the time; "when we know better, we do better." For some reason, however, I had forgotten to apply that truth to one of the most important relationships in my life. That realization lifted an incredible weight off my heart. I immediately sent a bouquet of flowers to my mother with a sincere note of apology for the coldness I'd treated her with and for the unfair expectations I had held for her. She had certainly turned her life around and deserved every bit of my love and respect. I also sent a note of apology to her husband, Bob, for my past behavior. I found Doyle on Facebook a day or two later and sent him a private message. Emotions from the past welled inside me as I remembered the anger, pain, and sadness this man caused my mom and me all those years ago. I chose not to dwell on those feelings. Instead, my note offered forgiveness. I didn't ask for or even want his apology. For my own well-being, I needed to forgive him—to set myself free from any hold I had allowed those memories to have over my life. It had nothing to do with him, and everything to do with me.

> *"There can be no future without forgiveness."*
> —Bishop Desmond Tutu

Suddenly, I was free! Free from the anger and hurt of the past, free from the weight of those memories, free from the pressure of trying to resolve past issues that really just needed to be released. For me, the true beauty of the forgiveness experience is that it allowed me to fully express my voice. I knew my voice before, but that tiny seed of bitterness caught in my throat. If you've even had an irritating, itchy catch, you know the feeling. You cough and "ahem" to clear your air passage, but the irritation just won't go away. You can still speak and even sing, but not with the same power and volume you could if your throat was clear. Well, for me, that irritation kept me from fully expressing the voice of my soul. I didn't realize to what extent those feelings bothered me until a few days later, when Pei remarked on the difference she saw in me. "There's more love coming out of you," she said. Wow. How long had I allowed those negative feelings to affect not only me, but also my relationship with my wife—and who knows how many others? I felt better, and just as important, now I am able to offer my absolute best to others.

If you think unforgiven circumstances aren't affecting you, read what Dr. Roberta Lee writes in *The SuperStress Solution* about why forgiving others and yourself is important to your emotional, mental, spiritual, and physical well-being:

"Forgiveness is essential to our spiritual nature because it allows us to release past hurts and failures from our minds. Joan Borysenko, a psychologist, author, and director of a spiritual mentoring program, calls forgiveness "accepting the core of every human being as the same as yourself and giving them the gift of not judging them." In essence, forgiveness isn't so much about letting the other guy off the hook as it is about letting *you* off the hook. When you forgive, you are no longer a victim of your own perceptions. You can change those perceptions: You do have that choice. In forgiving, you let go of resentment, anger, hostility, and guilt, all attitudes that directly fuel SuperStress. By forgiving, you protect your own physical self from the flood of damaging chemicals like adrenaline, noradrenalin, and cortisol that attend the stress response."

⚠ **Safety Steps**

Write a letter to the person you want to forgive (even if it's you). The act of putting your feelings on paper forces you to acknowledge the control you've allowed the past to hold over your present. Honor your emotions, then let go of those feelings of hurt, anger, resentment, bitterness, or fear. Remember: the only control your past holds over you is what you allow.

This activity is for your benefit. You don't have to give the letter to the person unless you want to. Alternatively, if it is helpful to you and your growth process, you may choose to have a "letting go" ceremony and burn the letter, or attach it to a helium-filled balloon and let it drift away.

Like the wake left by a motorboat, your past is a fading glimpse of where you have been, but it doesn't determine your destination. Dwelling on what happened in the past drains you of energy in the present. I hope you'll choose today to forgive others and forgive yourself. Set yourself free to live your best possible life.

Questions for Reflection

- What do you need to forgive yourself of once and for all so you can enter this next phase of life free from fear, guilt, or shame?
- Who do you need to ask for forgiveness?

CHALLENGES CAN REVEAL CLUES

No one likes struggles. And yet we are admonished throughout life to look for the good in our challenges. At church you may even hear the preacher say "consider it pure joy when you face trials."

Joy. Really?

I didn't have any joyful thoughts while fighting with kids at school. If anything, I'm sure I felt pain—physical pain from the blows, and emotional pain from not feeling like I was "good enough" or "normal."

Nor did I feel joyful when I watched my mom's boyfriend spin into drug- and alcohol-induced tirades during which he would scream, curse, and threaten my mom. It wasn't joy, but anger, frustration, hurt, insecurity, and sadness that ruled those moments.

When financial stress, infidelity, addiction, or irreconcilable differences rock marriage relationships, *joy* isn't the first word that comes to mind. When grief over a lost loved one hits us, or when we experience the pain of being laid off or fired, joy seems almost impossible to find.

So how can we truly be joyful in the midst of difficult circumstances? By remembering that struggles can produce character traits such as perseverance, maturity, and wisdom when we choose to learn from them. When we focus on the opportunities trials present—rather than the pain—we can find joy. That's how my friend Jennifer Finnegan turned a painful situation into a life of healing and hope.

FINDING JOY AND PURPOSE IN HEARTACHE

Jennifer should have been on track for a perfect life. She grew up in a religious home and was raised by two loving parents. With an intention to continue living the model life, she attended a Christian college and got involved in ministry work. She says she believed that if she "married a great guy and followed this rulebook, nothing bad would happen." So she married the right man and followed all the right rules—and was devastated when her life turned out to be very *im*perfect.

Early in life, Jennifer adopted the belief that to be loved, she had to be perfect. "My perception was that everyone expected me to have it all together. I felt the only way I was going to be accepted was if I performed well, so I became a master at performing," Jennifer says. She focused on trying to live up to the expectations she believed her parents, husband, and church held for her. "I was striving for that perfect look," she says. She wore the mask of perfection so convincingly that she forgot what really mattered to her.

Listen In

Hear Jennifer tell her story. Visit FYVBook.com and listen to the podcast titled: "Real Moms. Real Lives. Real Community."

But the internal didn't match the external. "My ex-husband had issues with addiction that impacted our marriage in many ways. We struggled with things I wouldn't allow anyone to see. I decided to hide instead of be real. It was dark and scary, and I would say I definitely lost my voice during that time. Inside, I was very, very lost on who I was."

Jennifer and her husband had been married for five years when her husband turned her life upside down with the words, "I'm leaving."

"It was a terrifying moment," Jennifer admits. The truth hit her: As a single mom of two young children, she had no job, no savings, and no way to support her family. "I lay on the ground and asked God to meet me—to be with me. I remember saying, 'I have no idea what direction I'm going to go in, but I'm going to put my faith in You.'" Suddenly, perfection was no longer the pursuit—realness was. "My marriage and divorce allowed me to see where God has called me to be authentic." During her marriage, she put off paying any attention to her unique gifts. In contrast, being on her own forced her to rediscover her true self. Tentatively, she took what I refer to as *safety steps*, small actions that moved her toward healing.

On a practical level, those steps included getting her children adjusted to life without their dad being present day to day, and taking a part-time job at a nearby factory to support her family. On an emotional level, it meant choosing to embrace the pain. It took her months to sort through the fear and uncertainty she felt. She grieved the loss of her marriage and came to grips with her role in that relationship and its failure. "Having to look at the parts in me that made me unable to move forward was very painful. Through that process, I started to get real. I realized I was a perfectionist, and that would have to stop."

Through self-reflection and by intentionally seeking out mentors and godly wisdom, Jennifer found her true self again. During the next two and a half years, she saved enough money for a down payment on a house. She also found a job in ministry as a school administrator—a position that better suited her personality. Money was still tight, but the job met her immediate financial needs. One day, a coworker approached her with an idea. She said, "Something needs to be done for single moms in our area. There's not a great emotional support system available." Clearly, with firsthand experience as a single mom who hadn't known where to turn in her community or church, Jennifer understood the need. But even as she promised to pray about it, her initial response was, "I don't think I'm the woman for the job."

Jennifer wrestled with the idea for three months. During that time, she says, "Single moms started coming out of the woodwork and telling me their stories." Although their tales of heartbreak, frustration, and fear tugged at her heart, she couldn't see her way around very real obstacles—like not having enough money to buy meat for her family, much less the funds to start an organization. One evening she pointed out her financial dilemma to God in prayer. The next day a woman came into her office and said, "We just butchered a pig and have all this extra meat. Would you like some?"

"That moment was a turning point for me," Jennifer says. "I thought, *God will provide. If He is guiding us there, He will take care of us.*" Despite doubts and fears that crept in during the following months, she left a paying job to embrace the idea of sharing her experiences to help other women as they struggled through the transition into single motherhood.

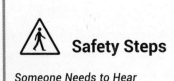

Safety Steps

Someone Needs to Hear Your Voice!
Write down the names of two or three organizations that could benefit from your experience.

Contact the volunteer coordinator, share your story, and get involved.

Jennifer used a dark time in her life to create a new beginning. Her voice, or at least part of it, is to bring healing, hope, and community to hurting women—specifically single mothers. Although she never planned to be a single mom, she used what she learned from that experience to bless others. She used her gift of ministry to empower single moms in her area with practical resources, support, and education. In 2012, Jennifer and I hosted a year's worth of Single Momm Radio shows together. The online radio program offers hope and encouragement to women around the world. (You can listen to the archived editions—at FYVBook.com.)

So when we talk about having joy through painful circumstances, we're not talking about enjoying the pain. How can we? No one enjoys suffering or trials. But we can take comfort in the knowledge that every struggle we endure can make us stronger and better if we choose to learn from the experience. Like Jennifer, you may discover that the difficulties you're facing now or that have touched your life in the past hold clues to finding your voice. Your struggles can become the catalyst for moving into a better place—emotionally, spiritually, financially, and relationally.

Interestingly, the events that take us to the lowest points in our life (business and career failures, the loss of a loved one, a financial collapse, etc.) often turn out to be both a springboard for greater success and a sounding-board for the voice within us. Zig Ziglar, Dave Ramsey, Dan Miller, and many other people whose wisdom is part of our everyday conversations, experienced devastating circumstances before they became household names. Ziglar failed as a salesperson before becoming a top seller in his company. He went on to share his insights with millions and build an internationally respected leadership and sales training company. Ramsey and Miller both experienced financial devastation before reaching successes beyond their wildest dreams. Each of these men chose to use their stories of personal disaster to empower others. You can do the same. No matter where you are in life, you can use your circumstances to catapult you forward rather than allow them to hold you back.

- You have a story others need to hear.
- Maybe it's a story of trial.
- Maybe it's a story of hope.
- Maybe it's a story of overcoming.

Whatever your story, I hope you'll choose to grow from the experience and then share what you learn with the world. God wants to use you as a beacon that shines a light of hope into others' lives. You are the solution someone could be waiting for this very instant. Someone needs the benefit of your battle scars!

Questions for Reflection

- What struggle or challenge are you trying to run from or forget?
- What would happen if you chose to purposefully learn from that difficulty and use the experience to fuel you?
- What wisdom, insights, or knowledge can you share from your own walk that can benefit others?

Turning Pain into Purpose

Colleen doesn't like to talk about her past. She's not in denial about the challenges she's experienced, but she chooses not to dwell on them. Instead, she lets what she's learned from the traumatic and dramatic experiences in her own life fuel her compassion for others.

For most of her life, Colleen lived in small towns. But after a difficult divorce, she moved to Atlanta. It was there, on the dirty downtown streets, that she discovered her voice and a winding path to healing.

One of the first things she noticed about Atlanta was the incredible number of people in need. "Everywhere I went, I saw homeless people," Colleen says. "I could see their hopelessness and despair; I felt the weight of it." The immense need tugged at her heart. In response, she began to spend her days in downtown Atlanta walking and talking with homeless people. "When people start losing things in life, they also lose their friends. Most of these people have no one to talk to," she says. "And because they don't smell good or look good, few people want to be near them." Colleen became determined to be the friend these individuals needed.

For the next few years, Colleen, whose background is in healthcare and education, left the confines of her professional career to spend hours each week working one-on-one with people on the street. She also volunteered in shelters and soup kitchens. Rather than stand behind the counter dishing out plates of food, Colleen grabbed the tea pitcher. As she walked around refilling people's cups, she heard countless stories. Over time, she developed relationships with "the regulars" that often evolved into coaching opportunities. She taught basic life skills to ex-convicts, connected addicts with recovery programs, and helped people find housing. Whatever the need, Colleen thrived on lifting people up. She had a need welling up inside her to share her voice.

What started as part-time volunteering turned into an intense lifestyle of full-time service. Although helping people through difficult times allowed her to find healing for her own past hurts, the role of giver became all-consuming. Somehow, her service had morphed from *desire* to *duty*—as though she was working to earn her worthiness. She devoted so much time to others that she lost herself. Strangely disconnected from the feelings that drew her to this service in the first place, Colleen stepped back and took an objective look at her life. In doing so, she recognized the fallacy of the belief pattern she'd fallen into—that to be worthy of love she had to serve to depletion. Rather than making her feel healthy and whole, the belief she had been operating on sucked her physical and emotional resources dry. "That's when I made the decision to take back my life," she says. Colleen immediately reduced the hours she gave to volunteer activities and searched for ways to use her skills to serve others and *herself.* She hired me as a life coach to help her narrow her focus for the coaching she wanted to do and find clarity about her next steps.

During the coaching process, Colleen made a Vision Board (an activity I'll explain in Chapter Six). In the center, she placed the words "urban missionary." If you look in a book of occupational titles, you won't see a definition there for *urban missionary.* It is a niche she carved out for herself. Colleen knew she held a deep a desire to help others, but experience taught her that going to such extremes robbed her joy. Not only hearing, but also listening to her soul's voice empowered her to take charge of the way she reaches out to others.

Today, Colleen combines her passion for helping people with her healthcare and education experience. The result is a more peaceful and joyful life that taps into what matters most to her. She works as a caregiver and patient advocate on a limited basis, a role that offers her the opportunity to nurture one-on-one relation-ships. Through our coaching, she discovered that her top strength is *maximizing*—or making the most of opportunities. That's why she enjoyed helping homeless people connect with the resources and help they needed. With a business partner, Colleen continues to use this strength by speaking to organizations and groups to help them find opportunities for growth. "We ignite hope, healing, and change so individuals, organizations, and communities can maximize their potential and success," she says. It's a harmonic blend that allows Colleen to serve and be fulfilled from a place of authenticity and strength.

CHAPTER SUMMARY

What statement or story from this chapter resonated with you the most? Why?

_____

_____

_____

_____

_____

_____

_____

How could this help you find *your* voice?

_____

_____

_____

_____

_____

_____

_____

_____

Chapter Four

WHAT'S YOUR PERSPECTIVE?

Your life falls in line with your perspective!

The stories in the previous chapter illustrate how your life follows suit when your perspective changes. Jennifer's self-imposed perception was that she had to appear perfect in order to be accepted. That perspective kept her from asking for help or allowing others to see the real Jennifer. Colleen, for a time, believed the only way to feel worthy was to give all her money, time, and energy to others. Problems arose when that level of selflessness completely drained her. She became unable to give because she simply had nothing left. When these two women changed the way they looked at their circumstances, what they saw changed as well.

Your perspective colors the way you see the world. It can allow you to see hope in even the darkest circumstances—or it can cloud your vision and make it impossible to see new opportunities. As you read this chapter, consider how differently your life would appear if you saw things from a new perspective.

A CHANGE OF PLANS

As a young adult, I believed I had to do something important in order to be significant. That's one of the reasons I planned to enter the military right after high school. I dreamed of becoming a soldier. I wanted to prove that nothing could hold me back. While life as a soldier was in my plans, it was not in God's. During my final year of high-school, the Marines, Army, Air Force, Coast Guard, and the National Guard all disqualified me due to my hearing complications. While it may not seem like a big deal to some, not being accepted into the military devastated me. On the day of our physical exam, as the new recruits were sworn in and given their first set of fatigues, I was given the equivalent of an "F" on my report card. My dream was cut short. Heartbroken from the denial, with my dad's help, I even wrote our congressman in hopes of finding another way in. That, too, was to no avail.

Without a plan, I wandered through the higher education system for the next few years. Like so many people, I made the expensive assumption that higher education automatically leads to a fulfilling life. If that were true, a diploma would solve everything. But for me, it clearly did not.

After college, I jumped from job to job every couple of years (if I wasn't fired first). I constantly searched for a career or company where I could fit in and make an impact in a way that made a difference to me. I participated in numerous networking groups and professional associations so I could meet more people and enlarge my circle. Each time I joined a new group, I secretly hoped to meet the one person who, with a wave of his or her magic wand, would transform my life. Another assumption I clung to was that if I met enough people, someone was bound to come along and save me.

During the 1990s, I worked in radio. In those days, radio personalities were like local celebrities. I enjoyed the feeling of being the life of the party. Unfortunately, I still didn't know my voice. My radio career tapped into my passion for broadcasting and communications and my love of engaging with and entertaining people. It also provided a vehicle for communicating and sharing myself with others. Unfortunately, because I didn't understand what was really important to me, I used that platform in disempowering, self-destructive, and downright dangerous ways. I wanted meaning in my life, but I looked for it in all the wrong places.

It wasn't until a medical scare brought me to my senses that my life began to change. I recognized my desperate need for faith in something bigger than me, and for the first time I went to church on my own. I needed answers. Inviting God into my life was a step in the right direction. Learning to view life from a perspective of faith certainly changed my behavior for the better.

Over the next few years, advances in technology put my radio career in jeopardy. Rather than wait for the bottom to fall out, I switched careers again. For a while, I found my stride working as a personal trainer for 24 Hour Fitness. For me, helping clients fit into their "skinny clothes" was about much more than teaching the mechanics of weight lifting or burning calories. I enjoyed empowering people to overcome perceived obstacles and reach within themselves to find the self-discipline and courage to make real changes. I loved that job, but unfortunately, not unlike Colleen, I burned myself out working fifteen-hour days. After a while, I had nothing left to give.

Rather than jumping immediately into another career, I focused on my education. You see, I was searching for more—I just didn't know what I wanted *more* of. Modeling the success of one of my personal training clients, I pursued and earned an MBA.

With the additional education behind me and student loans looming over me, I went to work in the banking industry. It didn't take long to realize the corporate world wasn't a good fit for me. For example, I took one job with a bank in which I was supposed to recruit people to fill cubicles. Instead, I focused on helping the candidates find roles that empowered them. To me, the people weren't quotas, they were uniquely gifted individuals who deserved to do something they enjoyed. You can see why my employer and I were at a standoff: he needed warm bodies; I couldn't stomach the thought of pigeonholing people without regard for their individuality and abilities. Beyond that, the job involved too much paperwork!

I left banking and took a different route: I began listening to my voice. I went back to school again to earn a master's degree in counseling. I knew I had a strong desire to help others. Just as I had done as a martial arts instructor and a personal trainer, I wanted to work with people one-on-one to encourage them to overcome challenges. I viewed counseling as an opportunity to do that on a larger scale. Only this time, my focus wasn't on helping people strengthen their bodies, but their hearts and minds. Initially, I put my counseling degree to work in the mental health system. That job was a better fit than banking, but still not exactly right. Counseling is a fairly slow process. In general, it's about looking backward and dealing with past issues. Now clearly, some of the activities in this book show that I believe in the value of looking backward—to a point. Depending on your history, circumstances, and personality, that process can take anywhere from a few minutes, to a few months, to a few years. There are times when extended counseling is absolutely necessary for a person's mental and emotional well-being. But remember when I said earlier that even good and socially acceptable things can drain you if they don't support and uplift the real you? Well, that was my situation.

I loved helping people, but my desire was (and is) to help them move forward—quickly. The mental health system didn't suit my personality or the vision I was creating for my life. Finally, I realized I had to be myself. For too many years, I made the mistake of pursuing titles and degrees I thought would impress others. At the same time, my true passion pursued me. In every job I ever held, voluntary or paid, I sought ways to help others be their best—even when "coaching" had nothing to do with my role. I couldn't help myself.

On the surface, my checkered career past looks like a series of unrelated failures. The reality, however, is that every job along the way pointed me to the career, contribution, and life designed for me—coaching people to overcome challenges; see their innate value, strengths, and abilities; and find their voice.

After years of running in the wrong direction, I stopped trying to shove myself into the neatly shaped box of a traditional career. I turned around and wholly embraced the person I was created to be.

Finding my voice took time. The same will be true in your life. But I promise, when you start to see yourself for who you really are, you will recognize your worth. You have something important to offer the world. The question is, Do you have the courage to look within and discover who you truly are?

Questions for Reflection

- Are you working in a role or volunteering in a position that doesn't support the real you?
- What do you see yourself as the solution to?

FINDING VALUE—DISCOVERING JOY

"I was afraid I'd look in the cupboard and find nothing there."

That's how Kim described the fear she felt about looking within herself to discover what she could offer the world.

"I never thought I had anything to offer. I'm not a doctor, teacher, or lawyer...I didn't think I had any really deep skill set," she says. Her belief that professional value came from traditional and extensive schooling stood between Kim and the change she wanted to see in her life and career. It also did a number on her self-confidence.

About a year before we began working together, Kim took a job as an administrator in a medical office. She'd been laid off during the six months prior, so the position felt like an answered prayer. But after two months, Kim knew she wasn't in the right place. It took ten more months, a lot of prayer, and significant soul searching before she gathered the courage to leave.

Kim had been hired as much for her people skills as for her organizational abilities. She was warned at the onset that this particular office needed cohesion. "The doctor wanted to create a team environment, and that was my area of expertise," Kim says. "My job was to help create a calmer, quieter, more joyful place." Unfortunately, the atmosphere in the office was quite the opposite. Gossip and backbiting were the norm. "Individually, everyone was great. But the collective environment was not emotionally healthy."

Before long, the stress of working in the dysfunctional office took its toll. "It was soul-stripping. Driving to work each day, I felt a tightness in my chest," she says. "I prayed all the way to the office that the day would go smoothly." Day after day, her stress level rose until her heart pounded with anxiety as she entered the office. The physical stress symptoms worsened until the only way she could make it into the office was to steel her resolve by clutching the doorframe, taking deep, calming breaths, and begging for a peaceful day.

Her husband encouraged her to leave the job, but Kim wanted to move *toward* something new, not just away from the challenging situation. She wanted a meaningful career and lifestyle not simply another job.

Kim's self-recovery/discovery process began by evaluating her strengths, personality, and unique skills. Eventually, she recognized a pattern. Regardless of the company or her job title, she says, "I always carved out a space to be a go-to resource for women, particularly moms, for advice about relationships and finances."

Safety Steps

Download the "What Do They Know?" questionnaire at FYVBook.com and ask your friends, family, and coworkers to complete it.

Throughout her adult life, Kim enjoyed learning about personality types, relationships, and personal development. "I learned techniques for becoming a better spouse, person, and parent," she says. Now, happily married to the same man for more than thirty years and as a proud mother to two grown daughters, she saw exactly how her study had paid off. It dawned on her that she possessed a wealth of knowledge and life experience she could offer others. "I realized I knew things that others didn't. What I'd learned about relationships through the years was actually valuable."

Another step for Kim in the self-recovery/discovery process included asking a few family members to fill out the "What Do They Know?" questionnaire. This simple and extremely helpful tool is designed to gather insights from those who know you best. It poses questions such as:

- What gifts or talents do you see in me?
- What types of people generally gravitate toward me?
- When do I seem the happiest?

Many times, my clients discover that other people's observations and insights confirm what they see in themselves. Kim says her family's answers not only affirmed her, but also raised her awareness of the gifts God created her to use.

Are you looking for a way back to yourself?

Start the journey today. Meet with one of our coaches for a complimentary thirty-minute Reflection Session. Visit FYVBook.com and complete the one-page consultation request form and someone from our team will reach out to you. Or, if you prefer, you can schedule your session over the phone, 424.888.FYVR (3987).

With a new sense of confidence, she set out to do what she "couldn't not do." Kim left her stressful, unsatisfying job and launched into a life of coaching, speaking, and writing. Today she uses her time and wisdom to help others grow in faith, gratitude and joy. She feels grateful for the opportunity to help a growing online community of women improve their lives and relationships. "Just knowing I am making a difference in their lives and marriages or relationships with their children is incredibly fulfilling," she says.

When Kim changed her perspective, she was able to see the value of her unique skills and gifts. With a commitment to finding your voice, the same can happen for you.

HONOR WHO YOU ARE

Kim found her voice by evaluating her strengths and putting them to work. She was lucky in that even though the office environment she worked in made her unhappy and stressed out, her employer recognized and appreciated her people-building skills. But what happens when others don't value your strengths, and instead focus intently on your weaknesses?

Think about how many times an authority figure in your life—a boss, a teacher or professor, a minister, a parent, or someone else you looked to for guidance—has pointed out areas of weakness (or difference) rather than celebrating your strengths. The overriding message is that in order to be successful you need to be well-rounded. The problem is, *well-rounded* is synonymous with *average*. Our homogenized culture celebrates average performance and average results. No wonder so many people have lost their voices. When you spend all your time trying to fit in, you forget who you really are—or, worse, you feel wrong for being yourself.

When you spend all your time trying to fit in, you forget who you really are—or, worse, you feel wrong for being yourself.

AM I SUPPOSED TO BE GOOD AT EVERYTHING?

Despite average marks in most of her classes, Mary was a gifted young lady. In fact, she excelled in one particular class out of her full load of six, working at two grade levels higher than that of her peers.

Not only did she have the intellectual gift for mastery in this subject, she loved the challenge that the problems presented and would often lose complete track of time as she used her wit and understanding to work through the course material.

Unfortunately, her teachers and especially her parents didn't share the same level of enthusiasm that she did for her favorite subject. And, while a steady stream of A's in this one subject were met with a slight smile and a nod, the attention was always placed on her average marks in the other classes. The driving message, sent by well-meaning parents and educators was: "For professional and personal success you have to be 'well-rounded.' Don't focus on what you're naturally good at. Focus on your weak areas."

It took a while, but the message finally got through and for the rest of her academic, and then later, professional career, Mary did just that. She focused on that in which she lacked natural talent and ability. As a result, she found herself falling further behind, while at the same time, becoming more frustrated with herself and emotionally drained in the process.

It wasn't because she lacked the intelligence or the energy needed for success, it was because she bought into the well-circulated myth that professional and personal success comes from being "well-rounded" and that the only way to achieve that is to spend the majority of her time attempting to pull up some of the weak spots.

Unfortunately, the push to strengthen one's weaknesses doesn't stop at graduation. In fact, it often escalates. Companies and organizations spend millions of dollars trying to coach their people to be someone they are not. People who are not designed for sales jobs are sent to "develop" the style of a closer; shy bookkeepers are enrolled in extensive training programs (often against their will) to help them learn to be more engaging; and those who are strong in creativity are shipped off to training so they can "change" parts of their *identity* and become more focused, better disciplined, and easier to manage.

Wouldn't it save everyone time and resources to hire the right talent set (notice I didn't say skill set) in the first place, instead of trying to decide in which programs to enroll people so they could "grow into" their new position?

It's amazing how frequently this practice plays out in homes, schools, offices, and networking groups around the world. If you're loud and outgoing, there will always be someone who tells you to tone it down.

If you're reserved and easy-going, you'll be encouraged to speak up for yourself, or be more aggressive. If you're creative and artsy, you'll be told to take life more seriously. If you've got a great head for details, someone will tell you to loosen up and take it easy.

The reality is, your personality, strengths, likes, and abilities are what make you both powerful and one of a kind. One of the essential aspects of finding your voice is to not only recognize your strengths and what excites you, but to honor and harness those parts of you.

HARNESS YOUR STRENGTHS

Rochelle, a chiropractor and former coaching client, recently got back in touch with me to share an *aha* moment she experienced while speaking at her church. The revelation culminated the self-recovery/discovery process we had begun almost a year earlier.

One Sunday, her pastor asked people to share how God's power showed up in their daily lives. Rochelle says, "I thought about volunteering but didn't because I thought, *I don't feel very powerful.*"

A few days later, Rochelle's pastor called and asked her to be one of the speakers the following Sunday. Not wanting to disappoint him, she agreed even though she didn't know what she would talk about. Still uncertain, she took the stage that Sunday and shared stories about her work and what she enjoyed most about interacting with patients. As she spoke, a theme surfaced. Difficult patients seemed drawn to her. People often came into her office with an almost belligerent attitude—especially if they had seen other doctors and were still hurting. Rochelle understood their pain, but, more importantly, she knew many of her patients simply wanted to be heard. They wanted their doctors to care about them. Rochelle did.

A light bulb flashed in her mind that morning: Her nurturing personality and gift of listening *blessed her patients.*

Her realization starkly contrasted with reviews she received from her former boss. Several months earlier, she had been relieved of her teaching duties at the chiropractic school where she worked. "My boss called me into his office and told me that I was too nurturing; that I needed to 'crack the whip' more," she remembers. "I was getting the same results as the other staff members, but in a different way. I thought I had been doing my job well."

Heartbroken, she looked for ways to change her personality. She wanted to become the person her boss told her she needed to be: assertive, outgoing, dominant. "I thought with enough coaching and training, I could become that person," Rochelle says. She connected with me through www.48Days.com and signed up for coaching.

We started her program with the DISC Personality Profile. The DISC reveals a person's strengths, weaknesses, and other personality traits. It's an incredibly helpful and insightful tool, designed to help you better understand yourself and what makes you tick. By assigning labels to different personality styles—*counselor, persuader, leader, advocate, promoter, creative,* etc.—the DISC profile identifies personal characteristics and patterns. This information empowers you to determine which careers may best suit you and the type of people with whom you work best. It also gives valuable clues on how to improve your communication with people (both at work and at home) who have different personality styles. If you haven't taken the DISC Personality Profile recently, I highly encourage you do so.

I always remind clients that no one personality style is better than another, but that isn't what Rochelle believed. Her boss wasn't the first person in her life to tell her she needed to change her personality. Years of feedback led her to believe that successful people were aggressive and dominant. "I signed up for coaching thinking I would magically be transformed into a 'successful' personality type."

What is Your DISC Personality Style?

D Dominance—direct, results-oriented, makes decisions quickly

I Influence—outgoing, gregarious, energized by being around others

S Steadiness—family-oriented, intuitive, likes feeling secure

C Compliance—careful, high attention to detail, enjoys learning

The DISC report is chock-full of insightful, clarifying, and empowering information. Some of the more helpful sections you'll find in the report are: *All About You*, *Your Strengths*, *Your Keys to Motivation*, *Relating to Others*, *Career Match*, and *Biblical Insights*.

Take the DISC Personality Profile at FYVBook.com and find out what drives you.

To help you get the most out of what you learn, after you take the DISC assessment at FYVBook.com, you are automatically registered for a complimentary thirty-minute DISC Discovery Session with a qualified coach.

Throughout her coaching sessions and in the months that followed, Rochelle learned a lot about herself and overcame a number of self-limiting beliefs. She left her position at the chiropractic school where her gifts weren't appreciated, and focused her efforts on building her own practice. But until she voiced her strengths that Sunday in church, she still felt like something was wrong with her—like she couldn't be really successful until she learned to be more forceful. In that moment, all the work she had done during the previous year to find her voice finally clicked.

"I realized that power is not tied to a personality type," she says. "Power comes from using the gifts God has given you to the fullest. I am an *advocate*; I'm good at listening. As a chiropractor, I am able to be quiet while my patients talk. I hear not just their words, but their hearts. I also realized I'd been guilty of not fully embracing who I am."

With that rush of insight, Rochelle immediately stopped trying to be someone other than herself. She evaluated the business methods she had been using—methods that were designed with more dominant personality and communication styles in mind—and started interacting with patients in a way that felt natural and comfortable for her. She listened even more attentively and allowed her patients to share their concerns rather than trying to immediately steer them into a treatment plan. The difference isn't the diagnosis, it is the way she connects with and relates to patients.

"Once people know you care about them, they will be compliant with their care," she says. That means they are more likely to follow through on her recommendations, complete the prescribed treatment, and, as a result, feel better. And, as we all know, happy patients are good for business and referrals, so I wasn't at all surprised to hear how her success immediately increased when she started operating in her strengths.

The most satisfying part of our coaching for me was hearing her say, "Now I can be who I truly am, not who I thought someone else wanted me to be."

Yes ma'am. That's what finding your voice is all about.

Rochelle said it so well: power is not a personality type. Power is functioning fully in whom you are created to be. You are your best, most powerful self when you make full use of your enduring qualities and unique traits. *Unique* means different, which means you're not going to be like anyone else. Despite what the world says, being different is a good thing!

> *Power is not a personality type. Power is functioning fully in who you are created to be.*

I know there have been people in your life (some with good intentions, and maybe even a few with selfish motives) who have tried to fit you into their mold—to get you to follow their rules. They want you to work on your weaknesses. But think about this: focusing on improving weaknesses takes time and attention away from harnessing and developing your strengths. People like Bill Gates, Richard Branson, Oprah Winfrey, and J. K. Rowling didn't succeed by trying to do everything or please everyone. Super-achievers and difference-makers harness their gifts so they can excel in their areas of expertise.

Lean into what feels natural. Embrace your best features. Harness your enduring qualities. Be who you are and let your uniqueness shine. Honor the gifts God has given you by using them to serve others. When you do that, I believe you'll take your success to a whole new level—a level that will surprise and thrill you.

Questions for Reflection

- What words or phrases did you hear from authority figures that gave you a wrong or incomplete understanding of your potential or possibilities? Were those people right, or were they just sharing with you the best of what they knew and understood at the time?

- Are you trying to change your personality to fit what the world says is "successful"?

- What specifically are you doing when you hear your voice?

CHAPTER SUMMARY

What statement or story from this chapter resonated with you the most? Why?

_____

_____

_____

_____

_____

_____

_____

_____

_____

How could this help you find *your* voice?

_____

_____

_____

_____

_____

_____

_____

_____

_____

Chapter Five

WHAT'S STEALING YOUR VOICE?

Devin Wyman grew up in the ghetto of East Palo Alto, California. At the time, the city was the murder capital of the United States and a fertile ground for acts of desperation. Devin's mother, a single parent for much of Devin's childhood, worked hard to provide for her four boys. Still, despite the long hours she put in each day, the family lived on the verge of poverty. Surrounded by hardship, Devin made a name for himself as an athlete. By the end of his senior year of high school, he had been offered $250,000 in football scholarships. He was set to be the first of his family to attend college.

Imagine the pride his mother must have felt the day of the press conference in their modest home. Local reporters from ABC, CBS, and NBC entered the Wyman home to interview the young football star. To Devin's surprise, the police followed the last TV crew through the door. In a split second, the truth of the words his mother continually preached rang clear: "What you do in the dark will come to the light."

Listen In

Hear Devin share his story. Visit FYVBook.com and listen to the podcast titled: "Second Half Comeback."

You see, Devin was a big kid with even bigger dreams. Being poor didn't fit his plans. His mother provided for his basic needs, but the lure of status, designer clothes, and nice shoes proved hard to resist. The crowd he ran with knew how to get the money for those things and offered him a way to afford them—by selling crack cocaine. A good day's work netted Devin as much as $1,500. He didn't see himself as a bad guy or even a criminal. Still, his mother had taught him right from wrong and he knew she wouldn't approve of his new "job." He went out of his way to keep her from getting suspicious of his newfound fortune. Instead of bringing his purchases home, Devin left his fancy new clothes at a friend's house, adding them slowly to his wardrobe. His attempts at keeping the secret blew up in his face when the cops showed up at his house that August afternoon.

Devin's arrest made the news as part of a citywide sting in which sixty drug dealers were rounded up. Judges didn't have leniency in mind. The police and judicial officials intended to send a very clear message. Four days after the arrest, Devin turned nineteen and shortly thereafter received a sentence of six months in jail and fourteen months' probation.

"I threw away a quarter-million-dollar scholarship for shoes and nice clothes," Devin says. "I made some wrong choices listening to wrong voices." Devin calls the sentence a "high cost for low living" and says going to jail was a critical turning point in his life. His mother reminded him, "No matter where you are, you can always hit your knees and ask for forgiveness." And that's exactly what he did. "I cried out to God for a second chance."

God answered his plea. Once he was out of jail, Devin enrolled in college and started playing football again. In 1996, the New England Patriots drafted him. Today, the Super Bowl ring he earned as a defensive lineman for the Patriots serves as a tangible symbol of second chances.

During the past several years, Devin has spoken to countless junior high and high school students, and prisoners around the world. His message is one of hope and, not surprisingly, second chances. He talks about setting goals, listening to the right voices, and finding faith. "I realized I can't change my past, but I can change my future," he tells audiences.

And each time he speaks, he hopes people will be inspired to listen to the right voice—their own.

When you listen to the wrong voices, you give away your power and lose your identity. In your case, the voices may not be those of drug dealers encouraging you to join in their rich and infamous lifestyle. But the fact that the wrong voices in your life aren't encouraging you to break the law doesn't make them any less of a threat to your emotional and spiritual well-being.

WRONG VOICES

What is the wrong voice? It's ultimately any voice other than your own.

Now you may be thinking, Wait a minute; isn't it good to get counsel from trustworthy friends, parents, or mentors?

Certainly it can be helpful to listen to varying points of view, especially from those you trust and who know you well. But always keep in mind that the people sharing their opinions don't have your personality, interests, or purpose. Naturally, their voices will differ from your own. That's why, at the beginning of every coaching relationship, one of the first things I say to a new client is, "Don't believe a word I say." It's the only rule I have. Of course, I get good shock value out of that statement, but, more importantly, it relays an essential point. Like everyone else, I have my own unique life experiences and beliefs. Just because I say something doesn't make it right or the *only* way to do things. My point of view and my beliefs are what I've seen work in my own life and in countless others' lives. Consider the ideas I offer. Test them against what you know. Try them to see if they work for you. But don't just believe something because I—or anyone else for that matter—said it.

Misinformation can come from people who truly care for you and have your best interests at heart. Loved ones share their fears and may even discourage you from trying something new in hopes of sparing you the mistakes or negative experiences they may have made in the past. For example, parents may unintentionally stifle their child's voice by persuading him or her to follow a career path without regard to the child's interests or desires. That happens not out of malice, but out of a desire to give their children good opportunities.

Other times, the wrong voices are pitching things that sound good, moral, and socially acceptable on the surface. Maybe you've heard things like this:

- All parents should be involved with the PTO.

- Children need the socialization they get in schools.

- Children thrive when they're homeschooled.

- Your family would be better off if you had a nine-to-five job.

- Your family would be better off if you stayed at home.

Obviously, any of the choices above could be right for some people and wrong for others. But if you associate with a group of people who all seem to think alike, you may end up second-guessing yourself when your opinions differ. That's why it's so important for you to know who you are. Recognizing the wrong voices enables you to avoid making choices that are wrong for you.

Some of the wrong voices you may be tempted to listen to come from people—well-meaning or not—who have different expectations of you than you have of or for yourself. As you read the next two stories, consider how others' expectations may be stealing your voice.

EXPECTATIONS

Susan spent her childhood swallowing her emotions. For reasons she couldn't understand, her father devalued her point of view and limited any attempt she made at self-expression. As a result, she grew up believing she had nothing important to say—and that she wasn't important enough to say anything. Her father's expectation was for her to be seen and not heard. Not surprisingly, those expectations and demands muffled her voice until she forgot she even had one. When she later married, she carried the lies her father had told about her lack of value and voice into that relationship.

Susan and her husband were separated by the time we started working together. Now, please hear me: I'm not saying their marriage crumbled because Susan didn't know her voice or how to use it. Marriage relationships are influenced by multiple factors and at least two parties. But could her denial of emotions and self-expression—her voice—have contributed to an unhappy marriage? I can't speak for her, but I'll turn that question over to you to reflect on in your own relationships.

Is your voice being heard in your relationships? Do you speak up for yourself, or do you expect others to automatically know what you need or want? Are you ever disappointed because your spouse or significant other isn't meeting your emotional needs? Before you get too disappointed by your relationships, answer these questions: Is my spouse (or are my friends or other family members) aware of my emotional needs? Am I aware of and honest about my own emotions, wants, and needs?

If your fallback response is "yes, dear," or "whatever you think is fine with me," how can your spouse or significant other know what you really want?

Ladies, you may be intuitive enough to know what your husband needs or wants—even if he doesn't fully understand it himself. Most men, on the other hand, do not have that gift. We need you to tell us what you want. Some of us need you to repeat it a few times before we actually hear and understand you.

After years of stifling her emotions, Susan is finally getting in touch with what drives her. The truth is, her emotions have always been part of her, but being forced to deny them as a child kept her from embracing who she was and what she cared about. Faced with the immediate need to support her and her two children financially as well as emotionally, she realized she had an opportunity to rediscover herself and create a life she truly enjoys.

WHAT WOULD PEOPLE THINK?

Expectations aren't always about childhood experiences. You could have had a wonderful childhood and still allow your own and others' expectations to hold you back.

Have you ever thought, *I'd love to...* be a stay at home parent, get a job, move across the country or to the other side of the planet, start a new business or a charity, write a book, or _____ (fill in the blank with your own wild dream), *but what would people think?*

You aren't alone. Jacquelynn fought against the confinement of social expectations when she decided to make a career switch from nursing to acting. "Nursing is noble," she says. "When I tell people I'm a nurse, they say, 'Oh, that's so great!' or 'You're such an angel.' But when I started telling people I wanted to act, the reaction was usually something like, 'That's what kids do.' It's easy to have a socially acceptable career. Acting, or really any of the arts, are looked at more like a hobby, not a vocation."

As Jacquelynn experienced, it can be tough to fight against others' expectations, but fighting yourself is far more difficult. The energy she exerted attempting to deny her dream left her exhausted and the stress taxed her health and her relationships. The day she finally gave into what she really wanted, her shift in focus and energy changed dramatically. In a very real sense, she had spent years fighting a losing battle. My encouragement to her was to stop fighting herself. "Lay down the gloves; surrender to who you are—and also to who you are not," I told her during one of our coaching calls. That moment, she said, "Tension and stress immediately left my body." In the following weeks, she created a workable plan to transition into her new career. She has since secured several professional acting gigs and is intentionally working to build contacts and pursue her dream.

Bottom line: If you're going to rattle your own cage, you can be sure you'll ruffle a few feathers. Don't allow others' expectations—or your perception of others' expectations—to keep you from soaring.

Success Tip: Find the Courage to Say No

One question I frequently ask at the beginning of a coaching session is: "What is one thing you've done for yourself since the last time we spoke that has helped you become a more powerful you?"

Early on in her coaching program, Jacquelynn—the nurse with a passion for acting—enthusiastically responded to the question saying, "I learned how to say *no*!" A friend asked her to run an inconvenient errand. It wasn't the first time the friend had made such a request and normally, despite the fact that it took her out of her way, Jacquelynn said yes to the opportunity to please someone. But this time, she responded, "No, sorry. I have other plans." For Jacquelynn, declining a request of her time and energy—two things she had been giving away to the detriment of her own success and well-being—felt *empowering*. Even better, she realized she could say no without the world coming to an end.

N.O. Those two simple letters can empower you to take back your life. Time and again clients share their surprise at the power of this safety step. "People don't all of a sudden hate me," is a common and freeing discovery.

↗ 7 Days of Self-Care
Having the courage and the will to say "No" is one of the tips we share in our ebook, "7 Days of Self-Care." Visit FYVBook.com to download your complimentary copy.

Respect yourself and your priorities enough to find the courage to say no to requests that don't line up with your interests, values, or lifestyle.

Questions for Reflection

- Have you ever said yes when you really wanted to say no? How did that pull you away from your authenticity?

- What are three things you are sitting on the fence about that you can say "no" to today?

BUSYNESS AND DISTRACTIONS

It's easy to get caught up in the busyness of just getting by. Internal obligations pile on top of external expectations until your day has no room left for you. That's when feelings of being overwhelmed set in and reality hits: *There's no way I can get all of this done.* And you know what? You're absolutely right. There is no way.

We live in a culture in which busyness is revered. The underlying message is that successful people have a lot to do. So, because of that, we stay "on" 24/7. Unfortunately, you can be really active without accomplishing anything meaningful.

If you're like a lot of people, the number of items on your to-do list extends well beyond what you are actually capable of completing in a week, much less a single day.

During a coaching call, a husband and wife recounted item after item on their to-do lists. Finally I asked, "What are you avoiding by keeping all these engines running?"

At first, they didn't have an answer. Busyness is tricky like that; it makes you feel good about doing something—anything. After further exploration, this couple realized they really didn't need to do most of the things they were allowing to consume their time and energy. When they examined the motives behind their behavior, they admitted to being fearful of some of the changes and introspection required to move forward with their goals. Self-preservation is a natural instinct.

Busyness is quite often a *tool* of distraction. We've been trained since childhood to occupy our time. The trouble is, when you are over-scheduled to the point of exhaustion, you have no time left for reflection. Distractions can keep you from looking within yourself to examine your vantage point, ideas, or feelings. Activities—especially those that serve no real purpose—provide an easy, socially acceptable way to avoid tough questions and emotions. When you're constantly focused on running from one meeting or activity to the next, you don't have time to relive dramatic experiences or delve into any type of spiritual restlessness or discontent.

Distractions come in a variety of forms, and they aren't always about looking busy or avoiding emotions. Sometimes they are simply the result of letting life happen. Remember Jacquelynn? She studied nursing as a fallback career. Her true passion was always performing, but her mother, also a nurse, persuaded her to get a nursing degree. "You'll always have a job," her mom reasoned. What started out as a safety net became a web that wrapped itself around her. Jacquelynn excelled at her job, yet lost touch with who she really was. Her bosses promoted her from one position to another, increasing her income along the way. Trapped in a *successful* and *profitable* career, she spent more time each year working as a nurse and less time pursuing acting. Twenty years later she realized that although nursing is a good career for some people, it isn't a career that fulfills her. It sounds counter-intuitive, but Jacquelynn's success kept her from listening to her voice.

Carolyn is another client who built a successful career only to realize at fifty-five, selling real estate was unfulfilling. She began the coaching process with the intention of finding a new job. However, as she worked through the homework and tuned into her voice, she kept hearing the word "dance." It showed up in her Vision Board, and when she asked her friends and family members to complete the "What Do They Know?" questionnaire, there it was again. She had long confined her passion for dance to the deep, untapped chambers of her heart. In her mind, it simply wasn't realistic to even consider a career involving dance. For years, she distracted herself with a more practical career choice. And yet, when she allowed herself to think about it, the idea of teaching people to dance filled her with joy. Looking at her Vision Board, it became clear that she had no choice but to take her passion out of hiding, dust it off, and see how she could use it to fully express her voice.

If you want to get beyond where you are now, if you want to experience healing, if you want your life to be truly fulfilling, you must get to the core of what it is you're trying to avoid with distractions. Make time in your schedule to reflect on what's important to you and your personal growth. Amazing things happen when you tell yourself the truth.

Success Tip: Take Time for Your Life

For some, the words *meditation* or *reflection prayer* conjure images of yogis or monks sitting in the lotus position for hours on end. If contortions aren't your thing, don't worry. My wife, Pei, is a yoga devotee, but even she will tell you that you don't need a mat to clear your mind. All you need is a little time and a quiet space.

While there is a wide range of effective meditation and reflective techniques, here's an easy way to get started:

Find a comfortable place to sit or lie down, then, for ten minutes, clear your mind and focus on your breathing. That's it. No extra equipment needed.

Once you get the rhythm of your breathing down, (it will probably happen around the count of ten or twenty), thoughts will begin to enter into your thinking. Choose a thought that brings you hope, love, and joy and explore through it. If your thought or idea moves you deeply, stay with it. Don't wander off. Examine it. Look at it from different angles, from the sides, from beneath, from above.

Be mindful and don't let yourself default to "How do I get there from here?" Enjoy your own company and let yourself be lost in the experience.

My client Glenn explains that, for him, reflective prayer and meditation are very closely connected—one often leads to the other—and both provide essential focus. "I've always been a dreamer," he says. "My ideas and thoughts wandered all over the place, like daydreaming. The silence and stillness of prayer and meditation help to center me. Random thoughts still enter my mind from time to time, but through practice I've learned how to let go and refocus my mind. I have been able to really get a better understanding of who I am."

One of the major benefits Glenn received from the practice of prayer and meditation is clarity. "I generally start and end my day with prayer and meditation. There are times when it's easy to get caught up with all that's going on. When I don't take time to pray and meditate, I lose my focus on the reality of my purpose—especially on busy days. Reflection brings me back to who I am; it helps ground me in my purpose."

Without question, meditation isn't as simple as it sounds. Sitting quietly for any length of time can be a challenge for some people. Combine a short attention span with all the distractions that surround and rise up within us, and meditation can feel like torture. But hang in there! Scientists say that people who regularly meditate learn how to handle life with less stress. Various studies have reported that meditation can help people experience relief from chronic pain, overcome addictions, lower blood pressure, and even slow down the effects of aging. Wouldn't those benefits be worth a few moments of quiet time?

Even if your car, bathroom, or office needs to serve as your ten-minute sanctuary, give yourself that gift.

Darren Hardy, publisher of *SUCCESS magazine*, refers to the practice of refocusing your mind first thing in the morning and at night before bedtime as "bookending your day." "It can be difficult, even futile, to predict or control what will show up in the middle of your workday. But you can almost always control how your day starts and ends," Darren writes in *The Compound Effect*. "All hell can break loose throughout the day, but because I control the bookends, I know I'm always going to start and finish strong." You can do the same.

Question for Reflection

- Without uprooting your schedule, how can you immediately carve out a few minutes to just be still and listen?

LIMITING BELIEFS

Others' expectations, distractions, and the wrong voices are all external forces that, if you allow them to, can diminish or drown out your voice. If you listen to those external voices long enough, you may start to believe them. And that's when things get tricky. Listening and valuing external voices above your own will shape the beliefs you hold about yourself.

Rudy Ruettiger Defied the Odds and Played for Notre Dame

Beliefs, either empowering or disempowering, are often presented to us as "rules" by people who care about us—usually as protection. However, good intentions can sometimes turn into self-imposed limitations. The movie *Rudy,* based on the real-life story of Rudy Ruettiger, provides a perfect example of how rules can be passed down from generation to generation, and if not questioned or challenged, can be accepted as *fact.* Rudy, played by Sean Astin, had a lifelong dream of playing football for his favorite team, the Fighting Irish of Notre Dame. In a pivotal scene, Rudy's father, Daniel (played by Ned Beatty), explains that being factory workers is their lot in life. They are spectators, not participants. Although he doesn't come out and say it, Daniel makes it clear that it's a family tradition to be poor. He worked in the oil refinery, like his dad before him, and like Rudy's older brother. It's a "good living" he explains, trying to convince Rudy to follow in their footsteps. You see, Rudy's dad and his brother bought into the handed-down rule that poverty-level factory work was all they could or should expect from life. That was their belief. Rudy, on the other hand, chose not to accept that as his.

In another scene, Rudy talks with Father Cavanaugh at Notre Dame, played by Robert Prosky, about his choice to follow his dream of attending and playing football there. Even Father Cavanaugh, a man of the cloth, tries to dissuade him saying, "This university, it's not for everybody." But Rudy believed differently about his plans.

"Ever since I was a kid I've wanted to go to school here. And ever since I was a kid, everyone said it couldn't be done. My whole life people have told me what I could do and couldn't do. I always listened to them, believed in what they said...I don't want to do that anymore."

If you've seen the movie, you know Rudy got finally got his chance. After applying four times, he was finally accepted to Notre Dame. He worked exceptionally hard, battling dyslexia off the field and training relentlessly for the football season. He earned a spot on the scout team— a practice squad that trained with the varsity team players—and in his senior year, he finally got his chance to play during a home game. Because he rejected the "rules" his family and others tried to pass down to him, Rudy Ruettiger was the first of only two players in the school's history to be carried off the field in victory by teammates.

Rudy refused to allow others' rules to limit his life. Today, he is a popular motivational speaker and corporate trainer on a mission to help teens and young adults achieve their "impossible" dreams. He heads the Rudy Foundation, a nonprofit organization "dedicated to the support and recognition of those who aspire to fulfill their dreams through character, courage, contribution, and commitment."

Dolly Parton Gives Back to a Community that Ridiculed Her Dreams

Dolly Parton, the leading lady of country music, is another outstanding achiever who could have let her community's "rule" system stop her career before it even began. Graduating with a small class at Sevier County High School in 1964, Dolly and the rest of her classmates stood before the audience and shared their plans for after graduation. Dolly took the stage and confidently proclaimed she was going to Nashville to become a music star. The entire room erupted in laughter and jeers. It was common knowledge in her small town that success on that scale was out of the question. After all, she grew up, as she describes it, "dirt poor," living in a one-room cabin with her parents and eleven siblings. The people from her hometown of Locust Ridge, Tennessee, accepted the belief that poverty was an acceptable way of life. Dolly believed something different.

Even before graduating from high school, Dolly began shaping her dream. She debuted on the Grand Ole Opry in 1959 and recorded her first single in 1962. The day after graduation, she did indeed move to Nashville where she launched into an undeniably successful career. She's since been inducted into no less than twelve halls of fame, including the Country Music Hall of Fame and Gospel Music Hall of Fame. She's composed more than three thousand songs and has an estimated $100 million in album sales.

Rather than shun the community that laughed her off the graduation stage, Dolly used her earnings to build Dollywood in Pigeon Forge, Tennessee. The theme park is the largest employer in the area. In 2011, the park celebrated twenty-five years of operation—during which time its employees earned a cumulative $1 billion. More than 2.5 million guests visit the park in a typical season (March to December) bringing significant tourism dollars to the area. Dolly's belief in her dreams empowered her to create opportunity not only for herself, but for thousands of others.

BREAKING THE BELIEF BARRIER

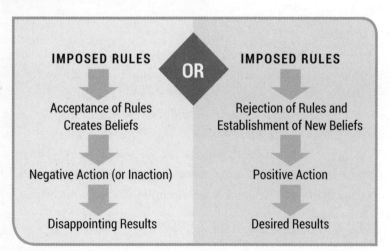

Whether your beliefs are positive or negative, they will drive your actions. Positive beliefs fuel positive actions. Over time, steps taken in the right direction lead to the life you want.

In both Rudy and Dolly's stories, the message from the people in their lives was "we're not good enough...neither are you." Their social groups repeatedly attempted to impress false beliefs and unnecessary limitations on them. Rudy and Dolly rejected the worn-out rules that their friends and family members tried to pass down to them. Instead, they created new, positive beliefs that affirmed what they *wanted* rather than what they had been told to settle for.

In a nutshell, they rearranged their beliefs to match their dreams.

You may have people in your life who are trying to impose their rules on you. They're the people who say, "This is the way we've always done it," or "What? This isn't good enough for you?" The question you need to ask yourself is: Am I willing to believe in their rules? If not, know that you have the ability to choose another path. It may not be easy to go against the crowd, but I'm betting you'll discover *it's worth it*.

AM I SMART ENOUGH TO GO FOR MY DREAM?

Your beliefs and self-image are shaped not only by what you hear from others, but by what you tell yourself. Thoughts about what you can or cannot do develop as the result of your experiences, your successes or failures, and your circumstances. My client Teresa, for example, believed she had missed her chance to accomplish her dream of being a physician.

From an outsider's perspective, Teresa's life looked pretty good. She had pulled herself together after weathering a tough divorce. The high-earning position she held in the finance department of a stable, international company provided a great income for herself and her two young children. But from her point of view, she could clearly see that her life was off course. She wanted to make a change, but the throbbing pain and guilt that accompanied her divorce made her skittish. In her words, she was "afraid of making another mistake."

As we worked through the coaching process, I asked Teresa about her purpose and what she really desired to do. It turns out she had known since the sixth grade that she wanted to heal people. She enrolled in college as a pre-med student, but around her sophomore year, fear and discouragement set in. "In college, I lost my way a bit," she says. Daunted by the thought of how long it would take to become a physician and swayed by the crowd she hung around, she decided to take a faster route to graduation and changed her major to finance. After ten years in the career, she was miserable. Even though she knew in her heart she wanted to heal people, self-limiting beliefs like "I'm not smart enough," "It's too late," and "I don't deserve a second chance," made such a drastic career change seem impossible.

As we talked, Teresa realized her past mistakes and failures should be cherished as learning experiences, rather than feared. Changing her perspective helped clear away some of the fog of those negative, self-deprecating thoughts. Soon, she began to see new possibilities for her life. Then, one day on her lunch break, a Google search blasted away any remaining doubts about her abilities. Teresa had made a New Year's resolution to get into Mensa. She'd taken some tests and knew her IQ, still, she says, "I really didn't think I was smart enough to be a doctor." On a whim, she typed in a search to find out the average IQ of physicians. The results surprised her. "My IQ was high enough that it was in the eightieth to ninetieth percentile of doctors. I instantly thought, *What the heck am I doing wasting my life here?*" She began immediately crafting a plan to study medicine.

> **What Are Your Possibilities?**
>
> To find your voice, sometimes all you need is a new conversation; one filled with hope, optimism, and possibilities. We frequently host Finding Your Voice webinars and teleconferences. To find out when our next one will be offered, and to reserve your spot, check out our calendar at FYVBook.com or email events@FYVBook.com.

The beliefs and fears that held Teresa back had traveled from the external and burrowed deep in her spirit. It wasn't until she chose to challenge her belief system that everything changed. With trust and practice, she learned to reach within herself and as a result, discovered a brave woman. Teresa had a choice: She could continue working in an unfulfilling job that made her miserable, or as she puts it, "I could take some risks and really live up to my potential. I realized I could accomplish way more than I was even reaching for."

WHAT DO YOU BELIEVE?

Teresa isn't alone in allowing her beliefs to inhibit her accomplishments. Everyone accepts certain beliefs as truth. These beliefs can be good or bad, true or false, effective or ineffective. Either way, your beliefs shape the way you live your life. Always.

- What you believe *about yourself* can push you to either explore new opportunities or to close yourself off from the risks of getting hurt and making mistakes.

- What you believe *about the world and your place in it* determines how you interact with others and what you allow yourself to experience.

Look at the following list of common limiting beliefs. Do any seem familiar? Have you repeated these or similar words as a reason for not pursuing your dreams or expressing your true voice?

- It will be tough.

- I don't have any support.

- I can't afford to take a risk.

- It will take too long.

- We don't need any more family drama.

- It can't be done.

- I'm too old.

- I'm not old enough.

- It's too intimidating.

- It's against the rules.

- I don't have the right education (degree, licensure, certification, etc.).

The underlying issue behind most of the beliefs or excuses—like those above—is the question of *deservedness* or *worth*. If you don't address beliefs that may be limiting you, it doesn't matter how many books you read, how many motivational seminars you attend, or how many coaches, therapists, or ministers you pour your heart out to. You'll remain stuck—held captive by chains you've put on yourself. Regardless of how unbreakable those chains seem, with a little faith and practice, you'll discover that it's possible to *control* what you believe about yourself and the world around you. When you learn how to believe differently about yourself, questions like "Do I deserve this?" begin to dissolve.

Self-limiting beliefs are like magnets under the floor that keep you locked in place.

FINDING YOUR VOICE ACTIVITY: TRANSFORMING SELF-LIMITING BELIEFS

Self-limiting beliefs are like magnets under the floor that keep you locked in place. You can't see them unless you start peeling back the layers. This activity will help you uncover self-limiting beliefs that could be holding you back. Once you understand and learn how to spot uninspired, hindering beliefs, you can then replace them with new, affirming beliefs. Creating a new belief system takes work, action, commitment, and time, but doing so is empowering! If you are committed to moving your life into a better place, you must be 100 percent intentional about the dialogue you participate in—especially with yourself.

Life Without Limits

Earl Nightingale said long ago, "You become what you think about." What we think about—especially as related to our potential, well-being, and success—becomes our reality. For example, if you're constantly saying, "I'm always late!" the likelihood is that statement has become true for you. You've told yourself so many times that you're never on time, that you really are late to almost every appointment or family gathering. Your thoughts and words make it a self-fulfilling prophecy.

Think about that "always" statement for a moment. Is that hundred percent true? Have you ever been on time? Probably so! Always and never are two very dangerous and inaccurate words. The truth may be that you don't have a habit of making punctuality a priority. Or maybe you try to pack too much into your schedule so that one activity or responsibility bumps into the next, which pushes back the next, until it feels impossible to maintain any semblance of a timely schedule.

Once you've identified your limiting beliefs, the next step is to create new beliefs. Verbally repeating your declarations of new, positive beliefs allows them to sink into your mind and spirit. Note: your declaration should consist of more than the opposite of your limiting belief. For example, if your limiting belief was, "I'm always late," your new belief should entail more than, "I'm always on time." That doesn't require any intellectual, emotional, or spiritual stretching. Instead, an affirmation for the former procrastinator might be, "I choose to believe I am important enough to give myself ample time to finish my projects." Or perhaps, "I choose to believe that it's OK to say no to others' requests for my time. I only commit to activities that fit into my unhurried schedule."

Take your time with this exercise; go deeper. Pull the negative, self-limiting beliefs out by the roots. Plant the seeds of new, positive and meaningful declarations. Then nourish those seeding beliefs by affirming them daily.

Step One: Identify Your Beliefs

Using the online handout/journal or in your notes create three columns and label them: FAMILY/RELATIONSHIPS, HEALTH/SELF-CARE, WORK/BUSINESS.

Now, take ten minutes to write down all of the beliefs you've come to accept as true in the three different areas. Don't edit or judge your thoughts, just document them. (*Rules* and *beliefs* are often so intertwined, it can be difficult to tell them apart. Don't let that bog you down. The important thing is that you begin to see and recognize them.)

> ↗ **Download the "Transforming Self-Limiting Beliefs" Worksheet at FYVBook.com.**

Don't give yourself a "free-pass" on this exercise. Hold yourself accountable to listing at least three-to-five for each category.

For example, a common belief that fits in the FAMILY/RELATIONSHIPS column is that to be a good friend, community member, wife, or sister, you have to sacrifice your time, energy, and values. Regardless of the emotional cost, you have to please others and fulfill their needs, wants, and desires.

Beliefs that many have accepted as *truth* that fit into the WORK/BUSINESS category, include:

- "Work is a bitter pill and is something that must be endured no matter what."

- "My work identifies who I am and the value that I bring."

- "It's not that bad. I should be grateful that I have a job."

And under the heading of HEALTH/SELF-CARE, you might list beliefs that put your well-being last on the list. Common in this category include: "It doesn't hurt that bad," or "The health and well-being of my children is more important than my own," or "If I take time for myself, other people will think I'm selfish."

Step Two: Challenge Your Beliefs

Now it's time to challenge the beliefs you've just listed. Look at what you wrote and ask yourself this very simple question: "Is it 100 percent true?" To get the full benefit of the exercise, I encourage you to do more than simply answer "yes" or "no." Explore through the question. Play devil's advocate. Consider what would happen if you broke or bent the rule (or belief as it were). Write out your response thoroughly. Answer truthfully and fully. I'm not asking you to challenge the person from whom the misaligned or corrupt rule originated. After all, they were just doing the best that they knew how at the time. What I want you to challenge is the belief itself.

Did any of the beliefs you've been living by prove to be false or inaccurate? You can keep your discoveries between you and God, write them in your journal, or you can share it in our Finding Your Voice online community.

Step Three: Find the Antidote

While awareness of self-limiting beliefs is a good first step in breaking their hold over you, until you have something of value to replace them with your mind will return to them out of habit. The next step in this process is to find an antidote for every self-limiting belief you listed. I promise you, there is a remedy that is waiting to heal every infectious belief.

Look for truths that contradict what you've been brought up to believe. You may find this evidence in the Bible or other spiritual literature, or in the writings, observations, and quotes of modern-day heroes.

Where the evidence comes from isn't as important as that you find and apply it.

Step Four: What Will You Choose To Believe Now?

This is where you begin the practical process of introducing new, more productive beliefs into your thinking and into your spirit. You do this by simply writing out what you now choose to believe. Consciously and purposefully establish new beliefs about you, your uniqueness, and your potential. These new belief statements should be personal and powerful, written in present tense, positive, and be passionate.

Teresa, the client I told you about earlier in this chapter, is now studying to become a physician. To follow her soul's voice, she had to reject and replace the disempowering beliefs that held her back. Below, I've listed a couple of her old beliefs followed by the new, empowering beliefs she wrote during this exercise.

> *Old Belief:* I'm not smart enough to be a doctor.
>
> *New Belief:* I choose now to believe that I am significant.
>
> *Old Belief:* I'm not worthy of my dreams because I've made too many mistakes in the past.
>
> *New Belief:* I choose now to believe that mistakes and failures are a learning experience to be cherished, not feared.

Now it's your turn. Write down three new beliefs (one from each category) in your journal. The point of zeroing in on only three is not to cap your creativity or potential, but to help you stay focused on developing a few new core beliefs. When your new, empowering thoughts become a natural part of your belief system, come back to this exercise and define a few more new beliefs.

I choose to now believe:

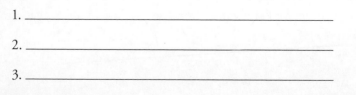

1. _____

2. _____

3. _____

Step Five: Speak the Truth

Once you have written your new beliefs, read them aloud to yourself. Over time, those words will move from your mouth, to your heart, to your spirit. I encourage you to meditate on your new beliefs at least once a day. Make it part of your morning routine or bookend if you will. Here is an easy way to incorporate it with the earlier meditation and reflective prayer practice we covered earlier. During this time, put your hand over your heart, close your eyes, and slowly and clearly repeat your new beliefs aloud. Visualize what the belief looks like. Let the words take root. Afterwards, go to your *Finding Your Voice Journal* and write for one minute. Don't edit your thoughts; just write exactly what comes to mind.

It may feel awkward at first to speak your new beliefs aloud to yourself, but wouldn't it be worth a bit of unease if the outcome was a happier, more powerful, and authentic you? The blessing of this exercise is that you get to choose what you believe.

You do not have to be a victim of the rules others have imposed on you. Take this opportunity to free yourself from self-limiting beliefs that have been blocking you from your potential. Doing so will allow you to fully enjoy the next phase of this process: discovering what really excites you.

CHAPTER SUMMARY

What statement or story from this chapter resonated with you the most? Why?

_____

_____

_____

_____

_____

_____

_____

How could this help you find *your* voice?

_____

_____

_____

_____

_____

_____

_____

I encourage you to share one (or more) of your new beliefs with our online community at FYVBook.com. There is incredible strength in numbers.

Chapter Six

WHAT EXCITES YOU?

When doctors drop the dreaded c-word, priorities suddenly become crystal clear. When Cindy received her cancer diagnosis, she immediately knew her life had to change.

For too long, she worked in an environment that stifled the person she knew she was created to be. After living behind a mask for thirty years in a career that required her to work against her natural personality traits and ignore her innate gifts, she wanted to let "the real Cindy" come out and play. Faced with her own mortality, the realization hit her: compromise and regrets were not what she wanted out of life. It was time to recover her true self.

Cindy took a family medical leave from her career in May 2009 to care for her physical health. In September 2010, with her cancer in remission, she decided to hire a career coach to help her find her way back into the marketplace. "I felt like I was in a rut, but I didn't know how to get out of it," Cindy says. That's when she found my friend and fellow coach, Rob Clinton. "I realized life was too short to not seek something to be passionate about, to not be joyful in my career, or to not have a good

Listen In

Hear Cindy tell her story. Visit FYVBook.com

boss. I knew what I *didn't* want." Figuring out what she *did* want took a little more time.

Through her coaching process with Rob, Cindy identified her strengths, what she loved, and what excited her. She describes her discoveries as nothing less than liberating. "I had been paralyzed in fear for what seemed like forever," she says. Freedom came as she uncovered her love for encouraging people. She understood that building real relationships and helping others had to become part of her everyday work and life—those elements are part of who she is at her core. She also remembered how much she enjoyed writing. Journaling became a cathartic routine that allowed her to privately, yet freely, express herself. Within a few months, she combined her love for writing with her desire to help others by sharing her experiences and hard-won wisdom in a blog.

Each step she took toward expressing her true self led to another. In her former career, she felt the need to be serious and matter-of-fact. In "real life," however, her friends knew her as a bubbly, warm person who gets quickly to the heart of a relationship. As she interviewed for a new job, she carefully considered the office environment and culture. She liked letting the "real Cindy" out—she didn't want to close off her natural instinct to be encouraging and caring. She thought, *I am not compromising this time. I'm not going back in the box.*

Although Cindy isn't my client, she has been on my radio show three times in the past couple years. We met when she was interviewing coaches back in 2010. Rob, who is an excellent career coach, was the perfect fit for what she needed at the time. Recently she told me, "Rob led me out of Egypt, and you took me to a whole new land." I say that not to impress you but to impress upon you the fact that finding the right coach and right friends is critical to your success. We all need people in our lives that will nurture, guide, challenge, and encourage us. I hope you, like Cindy, will be intentional about the people you choose to join you on your journey.

> ### Start Creating Your Support Team Today
>
> You never have to be alone in this journey. In the Finding Your Voice community, you will find a tapestry of diversity and experience. When you join the group at FYVBook.com, you can get involved in the conversation quickly, or, if you prefer, you can dip your toe in and see how it works first.
>
> Either way, we look forward to welcoming you to our family.

Cindy's journey evolved as she grew in confidence and in understanding of who she is and what excites her. Each time I've interviewed her, the "real Cindy" has been bolder about sharing her heart. In our third interview, she shared a thought that may be encouraging to you as you find your voice:

> "God brings people into my life that help me take that next step. There have been times when [I've taken major steps] forward, and other times it's been, 'I'm stuck and not moving anywhere!' It's a day-by-day journey; taking one step in front of the other, and watching to see what God does, and more importantly allowing Him to do what He needs to do in my life."

Cindy has since found a position she loves in a company with an environment and culture that suit her. "I get to be me for the first time in forty years," she says. When the mood strikes, she blogs about what moves her. She continues to encourage people, not only at work, but in various volunteer opportunities, and is constantly aware that life is too short to be anything less than passion-filled.

Download the "Identifying Your Support Team" worksheet at FYVBook.com

Safety Steps: Develop a Support Team

It takes courage to venture outside your comfort zone—especially when it seems everyone around you is trying to pull you back. If "bad company corrupts good character," the converse is also true. Jim Rohn said it this way: "You are the average of the five people you spend the most time with."

- Who in your life supports you *no matter what*? Ask them to have lunch or coffee and share your awareness, struggles, and journey. Chances are, your willingness to be real will embolden them to do the same.

- What events could you attend in the next few months where you can be surrounded by encouraging, solution-oriented people?

- Who do you need to spend *less* time with? If you feel drained, "beat down," or discouraged after an hour with someone, consider limiting your exposure to that person.

In his book *The Compound Effect*, my buddy Darren Hardy explains the importance of your associations—the people with whom you spend your time:

"There are some people you can spend three hours with, but not three days. Others you can spend three minutes with, but not three hours. Always remember that the influence of associations is both powerful and subtle.... Take a look at your relationships and make sure you're not spending three hours with a three-minute person."

Be intentional about connecting and surrounding yourself with people who lift you up and encourage you to be your best.

One more thought about your Support Team: Don't underestimate the value of an outside opinion. Lisa in Virginia decided to work with me specifically because I had no experience with her prior to her first coaching session. Here are her words, taken from my testimonial page: "I realized that there was no way I could do this on my own. I needed someone to guide me, push me, and help me along the way. Although I had been talking to friends and family about my journey, I felt I needed someone who didn't know me. Someone who had no prior expectations or experience with me.

WHY PASSION MATTERS

Knowing what really excites and ignites you is an essential step toward finding your voice. Conversely, not knowing your passion prevents you from living your authentic life and from effectively sharing your gifts with the world. The results of denying your true voice in the long term can be devastating. Kim and Jacquelynn, for example, expressed the physical symptoms they felt after years of tuning out their voice: exhaustion, excessive stress, and anxiety. Some people suffer from depression, and even heart disease and high blood pressure. Unfortunately, as my friend and mentor, Dan Miller, points out, "People pray, 'Please God, give me a sign. What should I do with my life? Should I stay in this job I hate or not?' They don't realize that the indigestion, heartburn, rashes, migraines, high blood pressure, and various other stress-related ailments are all signs. What more does God have to do?"

A passionless life leads to a miserable existence of mediocrity and "just getting by." You've surely heard the term "soul-sucking job." Well, when you aren't passionate about your day-to-day work, it can drain the life right out of you. When you're not happy, your work suffers. When your work suffers, your boss and clients notice, and, eventually, that shows up as lack of funds in your bank account. In contrast, Thomas Stanley explains in his book *The Millionaire Mind* that eighty percent of millionaires believe they would have never been successful had they not been extremely excited about their vocation.

Excitement is one of the key indicators of passion. More on that soon. When you wake up early because you look forward to the day, or when you lose track of time because you are "in the zone" and completely engaged in the task at hand—that's passion. For entrepreneurs and salespeople, this enthusiasm is especially critical. It's far easier to earn a living doing something you love. And the truth is, you're going to need excitement when the phone doesn't ring. Slumps happen to everyone. But when you believe in what you're doing and are *excited* about your work, it's much easier to push through those down times and into success.

"Without work, all life goes rotten. But when work is soulless, life stifles and dies." —Albert Camus

Money can be a byproduct of using your passion in the marketplace, but that isn't the only reason, or even the best reason to seek out what really drives you. When you do whatever it is that makes you come alive, you feel a sense of harmony and peace with life. Passion can add joy to your life, regardless of whether you use it as part of a paying career. Did you catch that last sentence? You don't have to get paid for your passion for it to bring you joy and fulfillment. Let me give you an example.

Rebecca LeCompte co-hosts the Blogtalk radio show, *The Imperfect Wives*. Although she studied and earned a degree in elementary education, Rebecca left her teaching job in favor of homeschooling her children and finding ways to make an even bigger, longer-lasting impact on children's lives. She knew that teachers only have students a few hours a day. Parents, on the other hand, have at least eighteen years to influence their children. To Rebecca's way of thinking, if she is able to encourage, equip, and empower parents—specifically moms—through the radio show, they could make an even greater difference in children's lives. By helping moms and wives be their best, Rebecca believes the influence they have is immeasurable. And so The Imperfect Wives prayer club and, later, online radio show was born with a mission to "inspire wives through God's Word to fight to save their marriages and to disciple women to be proactive in their faith by teaching God's truths about marriage and who He created them to be, allowing them to fully experience the life God designed them to live."

The group's effectiveness is witnessed in the marriages that have been strengthened and saved, and by the families who have become healthier and happier as a result of the prayer and study these women do.

Rebecca's listeners aren't the only beneficiaries of her encouragement. She takes the mission to heart, applying it to her family. Her goal is to help her children tap into what excites them most. For example,

Rebecca's oldest son, Nathaniel, loves math and science. But as his high school graduation date approached, he faced the question: *How am I going to make my life meaningful?* You see, his dad is a chaplain in the United States Navy. Faith, and specifically church ministry, are an integral part of his family's life. Nathaniel knew his life belonged to God, but felt conflicted about pursuing a career unrelated to traditional ministry. He had made the assumption that his family expected him to work in a church office. At the same time, Rebecca says, "Knowing his own personality, he knew working in the church full time wasn't a good fit."

Rebecca shared her son's concerns with me one day on the phone. Certainly, I understood and admired Nathaniel's desire to honor God with his life, but I reminded Rebecca that if we do what God has given us a passion for—and we do it with excellence—it's *all* service to God. With that reassurance, Rebecca felt confident to encourage her son to follow *his* passion. Today, Nathaniel is studying to be a chemical engineer. "He's found his niche for this season of life," Rebecca says. "He is the person everyone goes to when they need help with their studies, because he is the one who is *excited* about the work."

That shift in perspective—that we can pursue our passions *and* serve God—empowered Rebecca in a new way. With that truth in mind, she has encouraged her younger son to write, her daughter to dance, and her husband to write and record music. Each is following his or her own dream and using the gifts with which they have been blessed.

> **Help your child discover his or her strengths with the DISC Personality Profile. Visit FYVBook.com to learn more.**
>
> To help your sons and daughters get the most out of the DISC assessment, after completing it, they are automatically registered for a complimentary thirty-minute DISC Discovery Session with a qualified coach. Of course mom and dad are invited to sit-in during the session.

> ## Questions for Reflection
>
> If you've seen the movie *Chariots of Fire*, you probably remember the scene where Eric Liddle's sister was pleading with him to give up his passion for running and come back to the worthy life of a missionary. Eric's response is one that has been cited numerous times, "God made me fast, and when I run, I feel His pleasure."
>
> - When do you feel God's pleasure? (Be as specific as you can. Is it in a certain place? Is it during a certain activity? Who is with you? How often does it happen?)

WHAT IS PASSION?

One of the biggest fears people share with me is that they don't know what their passion is. They can't even begin to grasp what "passionate" feels like, other than how the word relates to romance...and that isn't what we're talking about here! *Excitement* on the other hand is much easier to understand. You know when you're excited, when your heart races with anticipation—like when you can't stop smiling and you feel thrilled at the prospect of participating in a specific activity. So as we discuss passion and how to find it, think in terms of what excites you—what gets you so fired up that you simply can't wait to do it. If you can identify those things, you're well on your way to uncovering your passion.

Before we get to the questions that will help reveal our excitement, let's get clear about what passion *isn't* so you have a better idea of what you're looking for.

Passion Isn't Your Role

You may be a leader, a volunteer, a parent, a daughter or son, or a sister or brother. Some roles are carried throughout life. Others are short-lived. In either case, even if the role is significant (like that of a parent) it doesn't define your voice or your passion.

Passion Isn't Your Skills or Talents

While knowledge of your competencies and skills is good, those traits don't equate to passion. *Passion* is about living a life that captures your essence and takes your breath away. To experience that, you must look beyond the mechanics and processes of what you've been trained and told to do. You will need to look deeper than the intellectual facts and figures you've been given to memorize and regurgitate. To find your passion, you must look to what excites you most and understand the desires of your heart.

Passion Isn't Your Voice

I've had a passion for broadcasting and radio since I was eight years old. That Christmas, I received a "boom box." Remember those? I can't recall anything else I got that year—the radio captivated me. From that day on, I spent hours at a time in my room listening to the radio, recording songs, and playing them back as if I were a DJ. I memorized the way announcers set up songs and what they said as they signed on and off the air. I was excited about the potential of communicating over the airwaves. And I still am. But as I mentioned in Chapter Four, because I didn't know my *voice*, my passion was misdirected. You need to understand your passion in order to fully express your voice; just don't mistake the two for being the same thing.

Passion Isn't an Occupation

Passion is bigger and deeper than any occupation. Certainly, it is wonderful if you can tap into what excites you and use that enthusiasm in your career. But a career isn't the only place passion can serve you.

"There is something that you love to labor for. There is a compelling in us that has been true our whole life." —Gary Barkalow

WHERE IS YOUR PASSION HIDING?

In my ebook, *Passion: Reconnect with What Lights Your Fire,* I identify places where passion hides. In the next few pages you'll learn how several of my friends and clients found their passion by searching within themselves and considering these four truths:

> ### ➤ Find Your Passion
>
> Help yourself to a complimentary eCopy of Passion: Reconnect to What Lights Your Fire. It's an easy, flip-through read with entertaining and insightful audio interviews.
>
> Here's what one expert had to say about the *Passion* ebook: "The captivating blend of questions, stories and audio interviews, stimulate the mind and stir the spirit." —Tom Ziglar, CEO and proud son of Zig Ziglar.

1. Passion is often something you would do even if you didn't get paid for it.

2. Sometimes passion isn't something you chase; sometimes it's what is chasing you.

3. Passion can be birthed out of personal struggles.

4. Passion can grow out of traumatic events.

As you read the following stories, consider which, if any, of these statements relate to your personal journey.

A Convenient Excuse

One of the top reasons people give for not pursuing their passions is God. Really? With good intentions, people have a tendency to say things like, "I don't want *my* passion, I want God's passion," or "I don't know if this is God's will."

While it's easy and perhaps even socially accept-able to delay action with questions about God's will, I've learned those questions can be a convenient excuse for not moving forward. Meditation and reflective prayer can help you find God's direction. It may also help to consider these questions:

- Do you believe God created you with unique skills, talents, and passions?

- If God created you with all your unique traits, is it possible that He instilled your passions in you because He wants you to do something with them?

- Could it be that you have a responsibility to identify and use your passions?

I want to encourage you not to ignore what God may be trying to tell you. Pay attention to the activities and circum-stances that excite you. How do you feel in those moments? Harness those emotions—don't stifle them.

If you're concerned about making the wrong decision, remember, few decisions are irreversible. Larry Winget puts it this way: "If you make a wrong decision, you'll figure out pretty quickly that you need to readjust your plans." If your decision is the right one, that will be evident fairly quickly as well. What's better: Wondering and waiting, or taking action?

Wherever you sit on the "Does God want me to follow my passion?" debate, you owe it to yourself and to your family to, at a minimum, understand what excites and moves you.

EXPLORE WHAT EXCITES YOU

Brittany, one of my coaching clients, is in the process of experiencing the joy of following her passion for art and creativity. "I've always enjoyed art, but never realized how important it is to incorporate it into my life," she says. Her role as a labor and delivery nurse gives her very little opportunity to express her artistic nature, so she took it upon herself to find a creative outlet. "It's a piece of the puzzle that was missing for me." She may eventually shift into or create a career that allows her to combine her love for helping people and her excitement for art, but she isn't waiting to pursue that which moves her. "Art makes me feel very empowered and free," she says. "I've started to draw and paint more, and, as I do, more and more ideas come to me. I've opened a well of ideas and energy and I know I just need to keep doing this." Brittany says her time spent in front of a canvas often turns into a time of worship. "It's a way to be quiet and be with God—a time to listen and reflect."

And really, that makes sense.

Thoughts, dreams, uninvented solutions, and ideas for creation were God's ideas first. The promptings and excitement you feel could be His way of getting your attention. *Don't ignore what God puts in front of you..* If you are enthusiastic about an idea, let that enthusiasm show and grow! Enthusiasm, after all, means "God within." With that in mind, consider that God could have placed your thoughts, dreams, emotions, and ideas within you as gifts for you to use for His glory.

Questions for Reflection

- What activity do you do just for the exhilaration of it?
- When do you feel completely at peace or joyful?
- If you're not quite sure how to answer those questions, what are some of the possibilities that could bring exhilaration, joy, and peace?

Nothing unlocks creativity like doing something that excites you.

IF MONEY WERE NO OBJECT...

When podcast expert Cliff Ravenscraft felt drawn to a complete career and lifestyle change, he admits to being irritated by passion-related questions. Maybe you can relate to the perspective he offered in an interview with me in 2011. He said, "I got frustrated every time I heard someone ask, 'What would you do if money were no object?' What a stupid question! No one can answer that question because money is always an object."

Early in life, Cliff believed he would eventually go into full-time ministry. Things didn't go exactly as planned and he ended up taking a job in his family's insurance business. For the first few years, his career advanced without a hitch. He enjoyed his job and earned a salary that allowed his wife, Stephanie, to be a stay-at-home mom and get his growing family on the path to a debt-free life. For fun, Cliff and Stephanie hosted a podcast about the TV show *Lost*. He loved using the platform to share his thoughts, and found the emerging technology interesting. He enjoyed podcasting.

Listen In

Hear Cliff tell his story. Visit FYVBook.com and listen to the podcast titled: "Real Passion = Real Profit."

Before too long, he discovered it was a door into a new kind of ministry. After talking about a *Lost* episode that contained spiritual undertones, Cliff received emails from listeners who had questions about faith. People shared their thoughts, fears, and doubts with Cliff, opening the door for meaningful and potentially life-changing conversations.

It might seem odd to say Cliff ministers to people through podcasting. Really, though, his ministry demonstrates the truth that it is impossible to rank the godliness of your work by how it fits within the walls of a church building. Ministry can be done anywhere. And I believe you can do *more* ministry by doing what you love. That's when people can connect with the real you.

Through podcasting, Cliff had discovered a way to live out his excitement and passion. But there was one big problem: Podcasting was a hobby, not a way to earn the kind of money he needed to support his family. He was doing what he loved, and for free. And money—or the lack of money—was an obstacle. Cliff lived down (not up) to the philosophy that work and play were opposites that couldn't coexist. Each day, he became more miserable at work because he couldn't focus his time and attention on what he really wanted to do. His overriding self-limiting belief was, "This is my lot in life: to suffer, pay taxes, and die." Stuck in the mire of that depressing perspective, he refused to entertain the idea of turning his passion into an income generator.

> Hope deferred makes the heart sick, but a longing fulfilled is a tree of life.

Cliff spent more and more time answering emails from his listeners and creating new shows—until the amount of time he spent on his hobby began to creep into his work hours. Weighed down with self-induced guilt over "stealing" time from his parents' business, he stopped podcasting for a week. Quitting, he believed, was the *responsible* thing to do. Immediately, misery consumed him to the point that he was barely able to get out of bed to go to work. He had no energy, motivation, or enthusiasm—for anything. During that one, long week, Cliff discovered an undeniable truth: *the only thing worse than not knowing your passion is ignoring it.* It takes more energy to hide who you truly are than to be in harmony with your authentic self.

Luckily, Stephanie recognized her husband's need to give himself over, surrender if you will, to his passion. Despite being a stay-at-home mom of three young children, she told Cliff she wanted him to quit his full-time job. "The kids need their dad back, and I need my husband back. I don't think we have a chance of getting that while you're working in insurance....Whatever we have to do, you have to quit your job." That was all the motivation he needed. He gave his notice the next day.

Was it easy? No. He still had no idea how to earn money with his podcasting skills. It took two years to get to the "eeking by" income level. Was it worth it? Yes! By the third year, Cliff duplicated and surpassed his previous career's annual income. More importantly, he is able to minister to 50,000 people worldwide each week through his podcasts. These are people he would have missed had he chosen to stay in insurance and ignore what really excited him. And although his desire to turn his hobby into a profitable business initially seemed almost frivolous, today he can authentically say, "What I do for a living is what I'm best at."

There is a reason you feel pulled toward particular activities, situations, and causes, but not to others. I like to think that it's a Divine reason. It honors God when you explore the gifts He has placed within you.

Questions for Reflection

- If no one was around to tell you what you could or could not do, what would you do?
- What would you do differently if you stopped trying to be someone you are not?

FINDING YOUR VOICE ACTIVITY: DISCOVER THE POWER OF JOURNALING

Many of my clients use journaling as part of the *Finding Your Voice* process. If you've already been using the online *Finding Your Voice Journal* or some other system to keep track of your answers and ideas, good for you. If you haven't yet, this is a great time to get started. The practice and process of recording your thoughts, feelings, dreams, experiences, and emotions allows you to look back over an extended period and find patterns.

For example, in this chapter we've looked at several places where passion hides. In a single day, you may not connect your excitement about an activity you did or an encounter you had that day with your passion. But when you keep a journal, you can look at past entries to see how, when, and why that enthusiasm resurfaces in your life. By paying close attention to the high and even low points in life, and capturing them in your *Finding Your Voice Journal,* the themes that emerge and link themselves together might surprise you. For this reason and for simply the cathartic nature of writing, journaling is an extremely valuable practice and one I encourage you to try.

As you journal, make note of each day's successes. Intentionally focus on what you're doing *right*! When you are working through a process of growth and change, discouragement can set in if things aren't moving as quickly as you'd like. Focusing your attention on what went well or on a positive step you took that day encourages you to 1) look for the good, and 2) keep succeeding. And, if that negative voice in your head starts slinging insults, you have ammunition—successes—that you can toss back as evidence of your progress. What a confidence builder!

GO AHEAD: EXPERIMENT WITH LIFE!

Have you ever watched a creative cook in the kitchen? A dash of this, a dollop of that, a pinch of something else...and the next thing you know, you're biting into a delicious concoction for which no recipe exists. Occasionally this kind of cook misses the mark: a cake flops or the sweet and sour sauce turns out a little too sour. In general though, experimental cooking works out just fine—and sometimes the combination of flavors blows your mind.

Working with the assumption that the food will be, at a minimum, edible and quite possibly amazing, the cook experiments with the ingredients, cooking temperature, and time in the oven. A periodic taste test and an occasional peek under the lid ensure the creation is on track.

The same approach that can work wonders in the kitchen can also work wonders in your life. Unfortunately, rather than experimenting and "taste testing" along the way many people approach every decision as if life and death hang in the balance. One wrong choice, and BAM! it's over. The pressure to make the *right* decision becomes so intense, the tendency can be to do nothing rather than make a wrong decision.

But what if you approached life differently (with a new belief perhaps) and assumed that by and large, most things work out OK and the things that don't generally aren't major catastrophes? What if you chose to see each situation for what it really is? A chance to grow.

If you tend to get stuck in indecision for fear of making a wrong move, try removing the drama from your decisions. Release the pressure to make the "right" decision by realizing that there may be several good choices. If you don't love the results of the first experiment, scratch it and go on to the next choice.

Take a minute to complete this thought: I've always wanted to:

Why haven't you done whatever it is you wrote on the lines above? What has been holding you back? How could you experiment with that idea?

Even small experiments can open your mind to new ideas and possibilities. By giving yourself permission to try something on a temporary basis, you free yourself from the fear of failure. It's OK if your experiment fails. Testing an idea's merit is what experiments are for. Maybe it will work. Maybe you'll love it. Or maybe you'll decide it isn't for you after all. You could study a subject that interests you, volunteer with a cause that tugs at your heart, take an internship or short-term apprenticeship, plan a trip to a place you've never been before, take on one client on a freelance assignment. You don't have to commit for a lifetime, and you might discover something that stirs your soul like never before. That's what happened for my friend Deby.

CREATING NEW OPPORTUNITIES

Two years ago, Deby's voice began to tremble. As doctors searched for the cause and a cure, her voice weakened until it one day it was completely gone. Suddenly becoming mute would be difficult for anyone, but for Deby the loss was exceptionally painful. She had been a singer and songwriter all her life and was just beginning a speaking and coaching career. She *needed* her voice to survive financially.

Deby and I have dear friends in common: Dan and Joanne Miller. One day Deby and Joanne were talking when Joanne said, "Deby, if you can't sing, and you can't talk, you've got to find another voice. So, what is it?" Deby chose art.

Through her pain and frustration, Deby heard a voice within her that told her to paint. She loves art in all forms and she is an amazing photographer, but she had never studied painting. At about the same time, Joanne began hosting an art class with painter and instructor Dorsey McHugh at the "Sanctuary" in Franklin, Tennessee. (The Sanctuary is an old barn on the Miller's property that Dan converted into a beautiful office and meeting space.) Deby lives only a few minutes away and

Listen In

Hear Deby share her story. Visit FYVBook.com and listen to the podcast titled: "She Found Healing in Unexpected Places."

immediately joined the class. "Dorsey is an amazingly gifted artist, but she's also gifted with inspiration. The first day she said, 'This is play. This is a discovery.'" Dorsey's instruction to the class was to remain unattached from the work—to be ready to rip it up and use it in another way. Dorsey removed all the stress from the learning process—something Deby desperately needed. Through the class and practicing at home each morning she discovered an untapped passion and talent. During a time when she couldn't speak, her art served as both a way to express herself and a source of healing. Over the next few months her voice slowly returned, but she knows she will never give up her newfound love of painting.

Questions for Reflection

- Are you willing to give yourself permission to "rip up your work"? In other words, can you experiment without demanding perfection from yourself?

- Without using words, how could you creatively give expression to your voice?

- What talents or gifts might you have overlooked or missed?

Although Deby would never have wished for such a trial, a number of blessings have unfolded as a result. For one, she continues to experience incredible peace and healing as she expresses her voice through art. Her relationship with God deepened in unexpected ways as she relearned how to play and enjoy the blessings He provides. And she has been able to sell several paintings and is using that money to send her teenage grandson to a school in England where he has experienced healing in his own life—all because she was willing to experiment with a brush and a palette. Deby's discovery of her passion for painting also helped her realize she may have other untapped gifts. "If this was hidden within me, what else could I have missed?"

GET EMOTIONAL

If you looked out the window the last time you took a flight you probably noticed the ramp agent—you know, the guy wearing earmuffs and carrying an orange flashlight in each hand. The agent uses those flashlights to direct the pilots safely between the gate and runway. Now, the pilot doesn't *have* to follow the ramp agent's directions. He has full control of his plane and can choose to go the way the flashlights are pointing, or go in the opposite direction. He has the *ability* to do either. But for his safety and the well-being of his passengers, he's probably going to choose to follow the agent's guidance.

Your emotions, like the ramp agent's directions, can be action signals pointing you in a particular direction. Society tells you to ignore some types of emotions, but I don't believe that's what God intended by allowing you to experience them. I believe He wants you to do something with what you're feeling. For example, if you're experiencing sadness, it could be His signal to grieve; if you're experiencing frustration, it could be His sign that you need to change your approach. Like the pilot, you have the freedom to follow the emotional directions God puts in your path—or you can choose to pretend you don't feel them and continue on your course.

What would happen if you followed some of the directions or guidance you're picking up through your emotions? You know the feelings:

- A sense that you should say no to a new project.

- A desire to try something new.

- Excitement about participating in an accountability group.

- The instinctive feeling that you should talk to a stranger (or avoid them).

By looking inward and trusting yourself and your emotions, you will often discover the answers you've been looking for. And you may find the key that will unlock your voice and new opportunities to use it.

If you feel happy, excited, intrigued, or joyful at the prospect of taking a particular action, try it! Remember, it's OK to experiment. Trust your instincts. And, if it turns out to be something that doesn't work, take what you learn from the experience and move on to the next.

Questions for Reflection

- How were emotions handled in your household growing up?
- What emotions keep nudging you to take action?
- How much energy would it save if you had a trusting relationship with your emotions?

FINDING YOUR VOICE ACTIVITY: VISUALIZE YOUR LIFE

I hope by now you're beginning to get an idea of what's important and meaningful for you. This activity is designed to bring that picture into focus by creating a vision for your life.

Oftentimes, the thought of having or creating a life vision can be frightening, sometimes even paralyzing. Part of the reason for that fear has to do with the way people frame the concept of visualization. People trick themselves into believing that their vision needs to resemble a fully-produced, three-dimensional, feature presentation; broadcast on the inside of their forehead. You know, I don't even know if that's possible— if it is, I haven't figured out how to do it yet!

In the real world, people don't come into the coaching process with a ready-made, IMAX-like vision for their future. We work with and build upon what they can see—the sneak peeks, the previews, the coming attractions of a possible future. As you begin this visualization process, you can do the same. Don't allow yourself to be held back by what you don't see; work with what you *do* see. The questions below will be helpful as you envision your future. Take a few minutes to jot down your responses here or in your journal.

If you were fully expressing yourself and being authentic to your voice, what would your life look like?

_____

_____

_____

_____

_____

_____

_____

Here are some thought-starters:

- Where would you travel?

- Where would you live and in what kind of house?

- What kind of work or business would you be involved in?

- How would you serve and add value to others?

- How would you look and feel physically and emotionally?

- What would your strongest values be?

There's a scene I love in the movie *Apollo 13*, where Jim Lovell (played by Tom Hanks) and his wife share a quiet moment after the excitement of watching Neil Armstrong take his first steps on the moon. Lovell covers the moon with his thumb, perhaps appreciating the perspective of exactly how far away the earth is from the moon and how impossible traveling that distance seemed only a few years before. Standing there in the garden, he says to his wife, "From now on, we live in a world where man has walked on the moon. And it's not a miracle, we just decided to go."

As you consider your vision, the distance you want to travel—emotionally, spiritually, professionally, physically, or even geographically—may seem impossible. You may even be thinking that it will take a miracle to accomplish your dreams. When you start to think that it's too far, or too hard, remember Lovell's statement: "It's not a miracle, we just decided to go." It's up to you to decide to create a meaningful vision for your life—and then to go for it.

CREATE A VISION BOARD

You have to see yourself in a better place if you expect to get there. The sharper the image is of what you seek, the easier it will be to recognize it when it shows up. One tool I've found to be incredibly helpful for bringing one's vision into focus is a Vision Board. I don't like to give a lot of rules or guidance for this activity because this is about creating a picture that moves, inspires, and motivates you. You can include whatever you want on your Vision Board. Here's what you'll need for this activity:

- A piece of poster board (even the top of a pizza box will work as long as it's clean!)

- Scissors

- Magazines

- Markers

- Glue

- A little imagination

My wife likes to print pictures off Google. Of course that's fine also. The key is to just get started!

Then consider your answers to the thought-starter questions I presented above. For each one, ask yourself: How can I represent that visually? Is it a word? Could it be a picture? Is it a color? Include shapes, designs, symbols, or phrases that are important to you as it relates to:

- Serving and helping others

- Your lifestyle

- Your values and guiding principles

- Your spiritual understanding

Don't limit yourself. Include anything that resonates with your voice and what you see as a necessary piece of the person you are growing into.

One client of mine, Diane, decided to do this Vision Board activity with her two teenage sons. At first, they responded to her request to sit with her and cut out pictures from magazines for their own Vision Boards as many of my clients initially do: They rolled their eyes. This is kid's stuff! But once they realized it was up to them and their creativity to paint the picture for their future—that it wasn't about following rules and coloring inside the lines—they got excited!

> **Check It Out**
> See examples of Vision Boards at FYVBook.com. Be sure to share yours as well!

The people who let their inner second grader loose and become fully engaged in the process experience similar exhilarating emotions. Many send pictures of their Vision Boards, and I love seeing and learning about what makes them tick.

The creative work and self-exploration of making a Vision Board helps you find clarity and pulls out the goals, dreams, and nature that exists within you. Once you have a clear picture of what you really want, you can create a plan to make those desires come to fruition. In the next chapter, we'll look at how to do that.

CHAPTER SUMMARY

What statement or story from this chapter resonated with you the most? Why?

_____

_____

_____

_____

_____

_____

_____

How could this help you find _your_ voice?

_____

_____

_____

_____

_____

_____

_____

_____

Chapter Seven

MOVING FORWARD WITH CLARITY, CONFIDENCE, AND DIRECTION

By now, even if it isn't crystal clear, I hope the vision for your life is coming into a more developed view. My prayer, too, is that you understand how infusing life with passion can bring more joy and fulfillment to your future—and your present. If you're like many people, though, you may feel a little discouraged or frustrated. You know, perhaps for the first time, what you want and what's really important to you. You finally understand, on a more definitive level, what drives you. The beautiful pictures and words on your Vision Board call out and invite you to move from a parched land of familiarity to one that is right, healthy, and abundant. And yet making your vision a reality may seem daunting.

At this point in the coaching process, some of my clients experience a roller coaster of emotions—excitement about what the future holds, fear about the change it will take to make it happen, stress at the idea of getting it all done, and joy at the freedom of being, loving, and appreciating themselves for who they are. If any (or all) of these sweep over you in the next few days and weeks, take comfort in knowing you're not alone. The tools in this chapter will help you find practical strategies to channel your newfound understanding in ways that matter deeply to you.

To get started, consider this statement: You don't have to (and perhaps shouldn't try to) get it *all* done at once. In fact, striving to achieve the perfect balance of home, family, and work may actually hold you back.

I can't tell you how many times I've heard clients and friends say, "If I could just get a handle on things and create some balance, then maybe I could sit down long enough to think about what I really want to do."

Does that sound like anyone you know? Maybe even you?

If you've been waiting for life to slow down so you can do what makes your heart sing, I have to ask, in my best Dr. Phil voice, "How's that working for you?"

Here's a news flash: Life balance is the myth of mediocrity. I know, I know. I just went counter-culture on you. After all, countless magazine articles, books, and talk show segments are devoted to the topic of creating work-life balance. In my experience, balance is just one more expectation people try (and fail) to live up to. The paradox I've seen time and again is that the more people strive for balance, the more obvious their priorities become.

Life balance is the myth of mediocrity.

Let me share Jeff's story with you as an example. Jeff contacted me about coaching because he wanted balance—or so he thought. Between his existing real estate business, his fledgling food blog, a family he adores, and all the little things that keep modern life in motion, he ran nonstop—and still felt behind.

Jeff wasn't looking for Zen-like peace, but he longed for a life with less chaos and more meaning. In his own life, the harder he worked to keep all the plates spinning, the more he wanted to pursue his true voice. For years, he had operated under the self-limiting belief that work wasn't supposed to be enjoyable. Additionally, he suffered from the all-too-common control-freak complex. His mantra was: *If it's going to get done, I have to be the one to do it.* Like a repetitive one-two punch, his beliefs kept knocking him back. As he puts it, "My life was full of distractions. And I wasn't managing them. The distractions were managing me."

Although he said he wanted balance, what he really wanted was to add some fun back into his life and become the man he was called to be. Unfortunately, spending more time on his hobby seemed out of the question; he already felt bad for not being able to give his family the time and attention they deserved. Held captive by his calendar, Jeff hesitated before signing up for coaching. Even though he knew he wanted to change the way he lived, he feared the commitment would turn into just one more appointment in his already overcrowded schedule.

When he mentioned the idea of balance in our initial interview, I had to be honest. I don't believe in balance. In fact, I cringe when people talk about work-life balance. Pop culture paints an idealistic picture of a Utopian environment where everything and everyone lives in harmony. The kids behave, get all A's, and are well-adjusted. Work is meaningful and fulfilling. And marriage and family relationships are all in sync. (Get real!) The problem is, while it sounds great in theory, balance doesn't play out well (or at all) in real life. Think about the tightrope walker at the circus. Sure, he can manage to teeter on that wire but, boy, it takes a lot of work! Every muscle in the performer's body is tensed—every thought focused on not falling. Just imagine if that tightrope walker had to wobble on the high wire for an hour, a day, a year, or for a lifetime.

Listen In

Hear Theresa Ceniccola speak about motherhood, faith, relationships, and working from home. Visit FYVBook.com and listen to the podcast titled "Are You Ready to be a Mompreneur?"

Our culture tries to convince us life is a balancing act. But is it really possible or desirable to sustain the level of physical and emotional effort required to live a perfectly balanced life? One of my frequent show guests, author, speaker, and founder of the International Christian Mompreneur Network, Theresa Ceniccola, rebuffs the illusion of balance. She so accurately makes the pointthat you can't *lean* into who you are, and be balanced.

Personally, I gave up trying to live a "balanced" life a long time ago because I found it so incredibly taxing and ineffective. Instead, my goal is living in a way that not only serves the greater good but feeds my soul and nurtures me from the inside out.

The questions I offered in response to Jeff's search for balance struck a chord with him—maybe it will for you too. Do you think life is really about balance, or is it about focusing on what really matters to you? What would happen if, instead of striving to live up to unrealistic expectations, you got really clear about your priorities and lined up your attention and intentions based on that focus? How would that focused activity change the way you experience life?

FROM VISION TO REALITY

In the previous chapter, you read about vision. Having a vision helps identify what matters most. Moving in the direction of what's most important makes it possible to experience a life of meaning—rather than one filled with mediocrity. Your Vision Board and what it highlights prevents the minutia of daily life from derailing your dreams. I hope you took the time to create your own Vision Board (see page 131); it will be helpful to have it in sight as you work though this next section in which you'll create a plan to make your vision a reality.

FYV STRATEGY #1: SET AUTHENTIC LONG-TERM GOALS

Are you living in the *afterlife?* Most people are. This afterlife isn't about harp music and clouds, it's about delaying *real* life. See if any of the following statements sound familiar:

I'll work out/look for a new job/start a business/take a vacation/
_____ (fill in the blank with your big goal)...

- After I get married

- After the baby is born
- After the kids are in school
- After I get my dream job
- After my kids get married
- After I retire
- After the grandkids are born
- After life slows down

You know what's next on the list? After you're dead. And you can't do much here on earth then. When you put off your goals until *after*, you aren't living fully alive *now*. Too many people confine themselves to boxes (house, cubicles, computers) and wait for the perfect time to do what's meaningful to them. While they wait for the afterlife, real life passes them by.

Even if you've grown accustomed to living in the afterlife, you have the authority to decide to live differently today. Your Vision Board provides the big picture of who you are, what excites you, and what you want out of life. Much of what you envision can be set in motion by going through the process we are about to cover: setting long-term goals and chunking them down into priorities or Daily Focal Points (more on DFPs later). Take a minute to examine your Vision Board. With your vision in mind, write down what you want to achieve, acquire, or become during the next three to five years.

1. _____

_____

_____

2. _____

_____

_____

3. _____

_____

_____

4. _____

_____

_____

5. _____

_____

_____

6. _____

_____

_____

7. _____

_____

_____

8. _____

_____

_____

9. _____

_____

_____

10. _____

_____

_____

What you've just listed are your big-picture or long-term goals. They may seem huge right now, and that's OK! There's no magic in thinking small, so don't.

The goal-setting process often uncovers valuable clues for finding your voice. Like the Vision Board activity, this strategy can help you gain even more clarity, confidence, and, of course, direction. When Brittany went through the goal setting process, she couldn't help but notice powerful themes and strong connections linking her goals together. Use what you learn from your goal list to refine your vision (if need be) and consider the people, things, and causes to which you want to devote your time and energy.

FYV STRATEGY #2: ESTABLISH PRIORITY GOALS

With your life vision and long-term goals in view, you're ready to take the next step and prioritize.

When Jeff created his Vision Board and goal list, his priorities quickly became evident: He wanted to spend more time with his family and build a platform as a food blogger and chef. He was a new dad and an aspiring entrepreneur. That was the season he was in. With that information, he was able to quickly evaluate tasks to see if they supported either of his main priorities. If a task wasn't in alignment with his top two priorities, he looked for ways to delegate it to the appropriate person. (See "Success Tip: Stop Trying to Do It All" on page 144 for advice on how to delegate effectively.)

Questions for Reflection

- Go against the myth of mediocrity. Instead of trying to balance out a laundry list of priorities, honor the season you are in by chunking down your long-term goals and listing out your top one, two, and at the most, three priority goals.
- What will help you accomplish your priority goals?
- When will you accomplish your priority goals (immediate—12 months time)?

While it isn't always easy (if ever) to zero-in on priorities, Jeff realized that if he wanted to become the father and entrepreneur he envisioned himself becoming, it was absolutely necessary. Over time, with a little coaching and some independent thought, he was able to shift his perspective and channel his time and energy toward his two main priorities. You can do the same.

I like to have three priority goals at any given time. And, like the gears that make the hands of a wrist watch move, I set my goals up in such a way that movement in one, triggers movement in the other.

Share your goals in the Finding Your Voice community. Let us cheer you on!

Success Tip: Stop Trying to Do It All

Jeff isn't alone in his (former) belief that if something was going to get done, he had to be the one to do it. The world is full of control freaks. If you're one of them—and would like to change that—ask yourself:

- Why do I feel the need to do it all?
- From what experience does that belief system stem?
- How would my life be different if I let go of that faulty belief?
- Does the thought of relinquishing some of my control scare me? If so, why?

In the process of finding his voice, Jeff realized he, like so many people, thought he had to control *everything* to be a responsible father and husband. He also believed that at some point he might actually get every task on his list completed—and *then* he could do what he really wanted. Through some self-exploration, he discovered neither of those beliefs were true.

"I was caught up in the idea that if I could do more, somehow I would feel better inside," Jeff says. In reality, the opposite occurred. "I kept checking things off my list, but I didn't feel like I was doing anything important. Trying to do it all built up anger and resentment in me."

Jeff evaluated his priorities, his season of life, and his strengths. Then, he sorted out the activities dividing them up by things for which he needed to be personally responsible, and things that could be assigned to someone else. He discovered the truth behind the phrase my friend Larry Winget uses: "Success is a process of elimination." By eliminating the activities that rob your time and energy, all you have left is success.

For example, Jeff realized that while he is great at executing a plan, he isn't analytical. So, while it felt strange at first to, for example, hand over the responsibility of keeping books to his wife, he says it was freeing. "The difference in my life has been all-encompassing. I can't even explain the peace that has come over me. I finally realized I don't have be everything to everybody."

"Delegation has been huge," Jeff says. "At first I thought it would be easy. Occasionally, I still think I'm putting the person out by asking for help, but in reality I know I'm empowering both of us."

Jeff shared an example of hiring someone to fix a sprinkler head in his lawn. "In the past, I would have just done it myself," he says. This time, Jeff contracted the job to a landscaper. "Instead of working all day in the yard, I got to spend time with my daughter." The simple shift from thinking he had to do it all to delegating tasks that others can do enabled him to reclaim time for his family and for himself.

"Now, I'm being deliberate with my time and taking care of my own emotional needs. I realized if my own tank isn't full, I'm not good for anyone else."

Questions for Reflection

- Have you learned to depend on disposable tasks as a form of distraction for yourself? Sometimes people keep so many bees buzzing in their head so they don't have to think about themselves on a deeper level.

- List two to three "no-brainer" tasks that you can immediately delegate or dismiss. How would *not* getting rid of disposable tasks keep you from fully expressing your voice?

SUBMIT TO THE SEASON

I've used the word *season* throughout the book and in the last section I encouraged you to "honor the season you are in." I want to take a moment to explain this concept in greater detail. As valuable as submitting to the seasons is for the farmer, this strategy can also save you from a lot of frustration.

Does a farmer attempt to plant, grow, harvest, and rest all at the same time? That's impossible, right? What does he do instead? He:

- Sows seeds when the ground and the weather are at the peak condition for planting.

- Weeds, fertilizes, and waters the growing plants— encouraging them to flourish.

- Harvests mature crops.

- Gives the earth and himself time to rest.

A farmer understands and submits to the seasons.

What would happen if the farmer tried to harvest when it was time to plant? Or rest during the harvest season? The results would be dramatically different—and not at all profitable. To reap a bountiful harvest, farmers must understand, embrace, and participate in the most important, valuable tasks for each specific season.

Success Tip: Be Present in Your Life

If you spend your day thinking about where you would like to be, you'll miss out on where you are. The blessings and the opportunities are in the *here and now*—they are divine gifts. We have the freedom to either ignore the moment or embrace it. Being present in the moment requires intention and discipline. It's tempting to get caught up worrying about the future or stewing about the past—but right now is the moment with the most power. Right now, this moment, is the only time you actually possess. I encourage you to use it well.

Admittedly, it isn't always easy to live in the present, but it is worth it. If you spiral into a worry session or realize you're overbooked, make a conscious choice to get back on track. Seasons change in your life, too, and they may or may not be related to chronological time. By that I mean the season you're in doesn't necessarily correlate to your age, or whether or not you have children at home. Certainly, these may be influencing circumstances, but the real determining factors are your priorities. If your priority is building a business, now may not be the best time to take a month-long vacation. If caring for an aging parent or a young child is your priority for this season, now may not be the ideal time to launch a time-intensive endeavor. Could it work? Sure. But you are likely to end up exhausted and unable to devote as much time and attention to either as you'd like.

The point here is that if you can take advantage of and fully appreciate the moment—you will experience more of the blessings that season has to offer.

Submit to the season and reap the reward.

Questions for Reflection

- What are three ways you can practice being present with yourself?
- Are you willing to do whatever it takes to be fully present when you're with others? (Examples: turn off your mobile phone during family time, unplug the TV in your bedroom, don't take your laptop or tablet to the dinner table, etc.)

FYV STRATEGY #3: FIND YOUR DAILY FOCAL POINTS

I used to spend time every Friday or Saturday to create my schedule for the upcoming week. Trying to live up to the myth of work-life balance, I spent a good deal of time making sure every area of my life was represented on my schedule. Inevitably, I'd a see hole, and say, "Oh, but wait a minute, I still haven't done anything in this particular area of my life." Then I'd try to balance it out and find another area that wasn't "balanced." The result for me was that rather than getting balanced, I became exhausted trying to make everything work.

I finally understood that balance truly is the myth and I determined from that point forward to only do what's important. Wow, that was freeing! Now I set aside time on the weekend to evaluate what I need to get accomplished for the coming week. Then, each week night, I write down my top three *daily focal points* (DFPs) for the following day. Because I am clear about my long-term and priority goals, I'm better equipped to hone-in on the DFPs that will move the needle.

I've already mentioned how journaling keeps you focused on your goals and progress. Now, I'd like you to add a new step to your journaling routine.

Most people crawl out of bed in the morning after they've hit snooze a few times. They stumble into the bathroom, look at their funky hair in the mirror and wonder, *What am I supposed to do now?* You don't have to be one of them. This new FYV step will help you begin your day with a plan of action.

Tonight, write down your three focal points for tomorrow. What do you want to accomplish? What "safety step" would move you forward? Commit in advance to devote your time and resources toward making your DFPs happen.

Writing down your top focal points before you turn in for the evening will give your mind the time and space it needs to contemplate and chew on them while you're sleeping; i.e. no extra effort. In the morning, review them and get the first one done as early as possible. The early win will super-charge your day!

When Jeff adopted the philosophy of living with intention and focus, he was shocked by the results. "I've never been so deliberate with my time before," Jeff says. "And I've never gotten so much accomplished as when I do *one* thing at a time rather than try to multitask."

"There are times when I've gotten away from what I've learned and I have to reset myself," Jeff told me. "That's when I know I have to get back to my 'dailies.'"

Let the Finding Your Voice team cheer you on! Share your goals and progress with the community at FYVBook.com.

Questions for Reflection

- Are you willing to zero-in on less, to accomplish more?

- If you were to fully embrace the concepts of priorities and focus, how would it change your life?

CHAPTER SUMMARY

What statement or story from this chapter resonated with you the most? Why?

_____

_____

_____

_____

_____

_____

_____

_____

How could this help you find *your* voice?

_____

_____

_____

_____

_____

_____

_____

_____

_____

Chapter Eight

ENJOY THE JOURNEY

Finding your voice is a process—a journey without a designated end.
There may be moments when you may get frustrated with a lack
of perceptible progress. Other times, you'll revel in the joy and peace of
feeling fully confident in yourself. But at no point will you sit back on
your sofa and say, "That's it! I've arrived. I'm as good and as happy as
I'll ever be."

No, you will continue to evolve every day! Life will present new challenges and opportunities. I hope you've seen through this book that even
as you grow and change, you can become more in tune with who you
really are and with what matters most to you.

That's how my journey has progressed. Day after day, year after year,
my vision for my life and my coaching practice expands. I've honed the
once undefined interest I had for "helping people" into a specific message: I want to help people—particularly women who have suffered some
sort of trauma or drama—clear away the clutter of life and rediscover
who they are—who they are created to be. My desire is to help them
find their voice.

Through my years of coaching, I've worked to develop an effective
process. I know without a doubt that if you'll immerse yourself in the
Finding Your Voice process, you will find greater clarity, confidence, and
direction. But even these proven tools and strategies don't work the same
way, or at the same speed, for each individual. For example, I told you

about Rochelle, the chiropractor I worked with who called me a year after her coaching sessions had ended. During our time together, she made positive strides. She continued to work through the process even after her last session. Then one day while sitting in church, everything just *clicked*. In an instant she understood the value of her unique personality style. Only, it didn't really happen in an instant, did it? She worked for more than a year, preparing her heart and mind to receive that truth.

For others, the improvements they make to their lives take an immediate effect. Jeff, the busy dad/real estate agent/food blogger who wanted that elusive "work-life balance" found something better. Because he was willing to delegate some tasks and focus on his priorities, he has experienced fabulous success with his food blog. He frequently gets invitations to new restaurants, and has been asked by several to critique their food. As his blog traffic and rankings increase, he is able to reach more people and take advantage of new and exciting opportunities. One such opportunity is writing for his local newspaper. "Doors are now opening that I never would have thought possible," Jeff says.

Brittany found a way to incorporate her passion for art without changing her job. As we wrapped up the coaching program, she connected with several other artistic friends to create a safe space for exploring their talents. She describes her life this way: "My job hasn't changed, but I have. My stress level has dropped and my life is calmer and more peaceful. This has been an amazing journey and one that has grown me spiritually!" She spends much of her free time painting and creating jewelry designed to inspire believers. Her husband offered to set up a website to display and sell her artwork and jewelry—and while a little extra money never hurts, it isn't the goal. Having enjoyed the thrill of being in sync with herself and her faith, creating is its own reward. "I've realized that I don't have to sell my art for it to be valuable and worthwhile—or for me to feel valued," she says.

And Kim, the mom and former doctor's office administrator, makes herself available to moms; building her platform. Her very active blog is a source of inspiration to women everywhere, and she recently released her first ebook, *Practicing Gratitude and Discovering Joy: 30 Days to a Happier You*. She knows from personal experience that there's no time like the present to live happier. You may remember that her courageous example inspired her daughters to pursue their own entrepreneurial endeavors, but the "butterfly effect" didn't stop there. "My husband and I have joined Toastmasters with an eye towards speaking to help others create stronger and more satisfying relationships," Kim says. It seems happiness and tuning into what really matters has become a complete family affair.

I share these stories of success in hopes that they encourage you to not give up on your dreams. Resist the urge to put time parameters on your journey. Instead, enjoy it! This is your life, you get to write the story you will live out. Make it as unique as you are.

EXPRESS YOUR VOICE

Before you close this book, reflect on what you've learned about yourself in this journey. Who are you? What do you stand for? What excites you? Take a few moments to review your goals, your Vision Board, and your answers to the Questions for Reflection. Based on all you've discovered and recovered, write your personal Voice Statement.

I've included a few client examples below, but please be true to *your* voice as you write your own statement.

This is how Brittany expressed her voice: "I help reveal others' true value and who they really are, *by being* creative and *by using* art to inspire and encourage others."

Kim shared this as hers: "To empower *moms* to build stronger and more satisfying relationships with their families, *by being* informative, thoughtful, supportive, hopeful, helpful, courageous, and inspiring, *by gathering and telling* stories with a moral."

Teresa defined her voice like this: "To heal *by being* generous, supportive, innovative, resourceful, insightful, and encouraging as evidenced *by the delivery of* creative and holistic responses to the physical, emotional, and spiritual needs of the poor, needy, and lost to bring relief to the world."

The suggested thought-starters below are just that, suggestions. Remember, *Finding Your Voice* isn't about following rules; it's about discovering and recovering the real you. If you prefer to write your Voice Statement in another format or style, that's perfectly fine. I want to offer thanks to Kent Julian for providing the ideas that helped me develop this Voice Statement outline.

I (ex.: reveal, heal, teach, empower, equip):

_____

_____

_____

_____

_____

_____

_____

Who do you do it for (ex.: moms, professionals, the poor, students, baby boomers)?:

_____

_____

_____

_____

_____

_____

_____

By using (ex.: story-telling, holistic responses, creativity, art):

_____

_____

_____

_____

_____

_____

_____

_____

By being (your enduring qualities—supportive, encouraging, innovative, resourceful, thoughtful, courageous):

_____

_____

_____

_____

_____

_____

_____

_____

Allow yourself the freedom and flexibility to write whatever speaks to you. You can always go back and wordsmith it as needed.

A PERSONAL INVITATION

Now that you have an understanding or an idea of the components that are in your unique voice, I hope you'll start using it. I invite you to engage with me online at FYVBook.com and get involved in our vibrant *Finding Your Voice* community. My desire is that you'll use what you've learned to create the best possible life for yourself. If you'd like more personal guidance, why not sign up for a complimentary coaching consultation with me or someone on the *Finding Your Voice* Coaching Team. Let's work together to figure out how to make your voice sing.

Do yourself and the world a favor. Don't put your book and notes away. Instead, put in motion the thoughts, emotions, and dreams you may have given birth to or revived during this process. The world needs what you have to offer. Your insight, wisdom, and experience are the missing piece that someone is looking for right now. Please share your gift. Don't deny them or yourself of that blessing.

When you find your voice, you find a way back to yourself.

MORE TOOLS AND RESOURCES TO HELP YOU FIND YOUR VOICE

FYVBook.com offers access to a wealth of resources to help you find your voice. Additionally, you'll connect with a supportive community of people who, like you, are on this journey of self-recovery. I hope to see you there!

One-on-One Coaching

Like my friend Ron McIntosh, author of *The Greatest Secret*, said on one of my podcasts, "If there were ever a time when we needed to know our voice, it's now."

Let's put what you've learned into practice. This book will save you $300 off the tuition of any coaching or live event package. Plus, as an added bonus, you can pass along the discounted rate to your family and office. Fill out the consultation request form at FYVBook.com or call 424.888.FYVR (3987) for more details and to schedule a complimentary Reflection Session.

Finding Your Voice Podcast

While having a coach can be practical and pivotal for moving forward in your path of development, sometimes, all you need is a sounding board and a second opinion. When those moments pop up, keep our number and email handy.

Ask your questions on the recorded listener line and we will answer as many as we can on upcoming Finding Your Voice shows. Finding Your Voice listener line: 424.888.FYVR (3987).

If it would be easier for you to ask your questions live, just let us know and our team will be in touch.

Finding Your Voice email: questions@findingyourvoiceradio.com.

Finding Your Voice Online Community and Events

There is an old Japanese proverb that says, "None of us is as smart as all of us." I've personally seen magic enter the room when people put their heads together and focus on ideas and possibilities. Regardless of where you are in the Finding Your Voice journey, you and a friend are invited to join our seasonal brainstorming calls. You'll find the live sessions to be filled with energy, excitement, creativity, and fun. Check the calendar at FYVBook.com for dates and times of upcoming events.

While you're there, click on the link to connect with the online community on Facebook.

DISC Personality Assessment

Discover what drives you. Take the DISC Personality Assessment online. You will receive an in-depth report that explains your strengths and communication styles. Your assessment includes a complimentary thirty-minute Discovery Session. After you receive the report, someone from the Finding Your Voice team will contact you to schedule your personal, complimentary session.

Finding Your Voice Journal

Download your *Finding Your Voice Journal* at FYVBook.com. Record your progress as you (re)discover the real you.

Finding Your Voice Self-Study and Coaching Curriculum

All of the tools mentioned in *Finding Your Voice* are available as free downloads at FYVBook.com.

ABOUT THE AUTHOR

Joel Boggess is the go-to guy for clarity, confidence, and direction. As a life and career coach, radio host and motivational speaker, Joel helps men and women find that "something more" they desire for their lives. His passion and expertise is teaching people how to connect with who they really are, what excites them, and what they stand for.

"Once you get clarity about who you are created to be and learn how to tune into your inner voice, making the right career, family, and life decisions becomes easy," Joel explains.

Originally from San Antonio, Texas, Joel earned his undergraduate degree at Texas Tech University. In his personal journey to find his voice, he later went back to school and earn and MBA as well as a master's degree in counseling from Amberton University.

He and his wife Pei live in the Dallas/Fort Worth area, and have two Golden Retrievers, Bubba and Jake.

NOTES